Dr. Kathy Koch wants parents to know that the [...] they excel in the classroom or not. By providing [...] eight kinds of intelligences and how to nurture [...] Kathy is helping pave the way for a lifetime of success and fulfillment [...] learn to master their unique skills and God-given callings.

Jim Daly, president, Focus on the Family

As the mom of an ADD son who has always felt "not smart," I found my eyes filling with grateful tears as I discovered all the ways I can *prove* to him that he *is* smart, and here is how. Kathy: our family is in your debt.

Shaunti Feldhahn, social researcher, national speaker, author

The contents of this book were absolutely revolutionary for my family. Understanding how God created each of us to learn and process the world was so helpful in allowing us to accept our differences and encourage one another. Dr. Kathy really understands kids.

Jill Savage, coauthor of *No More Perfect Kids*, founder and CEO of Hearts at Home

If you want to see your child through a clearer lens and be better prepared to not only bring the best out of them each day but aim them at a much more meaningful future, read this book from cover to cover.

Dr. Tim Kimmel, author, *Grace-Based Parenting*

Dr. Koch has created a practical, positive, and proactive way to help *everyone* feel smart and be smarter by achieving their God-given potential. If you have ever felt less than smart, or know someone who has, this book is the key to unlocking their future.

Pam Farrel, author, *Men Are Like Waffles, Women Are Like Spaghetti*

I have personally witnessed literal life transformation as hundreds have finally discovered they are truly smart. Every church and every church leader concerned about the next generation must find a way to get *8 Great Smarts* into the hands of parents, grandparents, and guardians.

Patrick Payton, founding pastor, Stonegate Fellowship, Midland, TX

8 Great Smarts is packed with practical, hands-on guidance and will help parents tailor their parenting style to bring out the best in the unique kids God has given them.

Todd Cartmell, PsyD., clinical psychologist, author of *8 Simple Tools for Raising Great Kids*

If you long to better understand your child's learning style so you can better train him or her to do and be all God intended, read Kathy's book from cover to cover.

Susie Larson, radio host, national speaker, author of *Your Sacred Yes* and *Growing Grateful Kids*

Dr. Kathy Koch has helped me redefine what "smart" looks like. I guarantee this book will open your eyes to see your child's innate strengths. Your kids will soar as you focus on their brand of smart!

Arlene Pellicane, author, *31 Days to Becoming a Happy Mom* and coauthor, *Growing Up Social*

Kathy Koch explains multiple intelligences and how these strengths affect academics, relationships, character, and Christian growth. Her insights can help parents equip their children to flourish.

Kathy Kuhl, speaker, author, *Homeschooling Your Struggling Learner.* LearnDifferently.com

8 Great Smarts should be required reading for all parents! It is both practical and profound, and holds the promise of being truly life-changing for those children who are blessed to have their parents incorporate its wisdom.

Brennan and Mary Jo Dean, founders, Great Homeschool Conventions

Not only will this book give parents tools to recognize the unique genius of each of their children, it gives them something even more valuable: hope. Hope that each child can find the smart that is uniquely theirs.

Kathi Lipp, author, *I Need Some Help Here: Hope for When Your Kids Don't Go According to Plan*

Dr. Kathy clearly articulates how to nurture your children to their fullest potential. In a world where children are bombarded with who they should be, this book guides you to an understanding of who the Creator designed them to be.

Robyn Terwilleger, chief administrator, International Community School, Winter Park, FL

8GREAT SMARTS

Discover and Nurture Your Child's Intelligences

KATHY KOCH, PhD

MOODY PUBLISHERS
CHICAGO

Edited by Elizabeth Cody Newenhuyse
Interior design: Puckett Smartt
Cover design: Erik M. Peterson
Cover image of brain icon copyright © 2015 by Daniel Rodríguez Quintana/Stocksy (69957685). All rights reserved.

Library of Congress Cataloging-in-Publication Data

Names: Koch, Kathy, author.
Title: 8 great smarts : discover and nurture your child's intelligences /
   Kathy Koch, PhD ; foreword by John Stonestreet.
Other titles: How am I smart? | Eight great smarts
Description: Revised and updated edition. | Chicago : Moody Publishers, 2016.
   | Revised and updated edition of the author's How am I smart?, 2007. |
   Includes bibliographical references.
Identifiers: LCCN 2015040617 | ISBN 9780802413598 (paperback)
Subjects: LCSH: Multiple intelligences--Religious aspects--Christianity. |
   Intellect--Religious aspects--Christianity. | Multiple intelligences. |
   BISAC: FAMILY & RELATIONSHIPS / Parenting / General. | PSYCHOLOGY /
   Personality. | RELIGION / Christian Life / Family.
Classification: LCC BV4509.5 .K64 2016 | DDC 153.9--dc23 LC record available at http://
lccn.loc.gov/2015040617

We hope you enjoy this book from Moody Publishers. Our goal is to provide high-quality, thought-provoking books and products that connect truth to your real needs and challenges. For more information on other books and products written and produced from a biblical perspective, go to www.moodypublishers.com or write to:

Moody Publishers
820 N. LaSalle Boulevard
Chicago, IL 60610

7 9 10 8

Printed in the United States of America

I dedicate this book to my grandparents who
celebrated me, my brother, and our cousins
consistently and personally.
They affirmed us and inspired us
to become who God created us to be.
I'm grateful for all grandparents doing the same
for their grandchildren today.

CONTENTS

FOREWORD

I travel often for work, and my daughters know that they will join me for a "daddy trip" once or twice a year. From the moment Anna, our middle daughter, wakes up on the morning of her "daddy trip"—no matter how early it is—until we return home a few days later, she is talking. She talks to whoever will listen: me, flight attendants, strangers, even herself. She's "word smart" (and, nearly as much, "people smart").

Recently, our youngest daughter, Ali, joined me for a "daddy trip" to Washington, DC. She has far more energy than I, and constantly needs to be doing something. With an extra afternoon to spare, we visited the Smithsonian Museum of Natural History. She loved seeing the exhibits but when, near the end of the day, we found a room with rock and fossil specimens you could choose, touch, handle, and examine under a microscope, she was thoroughly captivated. One specimen after another after another was lifted out of the box, examined, and returned. Had we found that room earlier, we wouldn't have made it to any other exhibits. She's "nature smart" and "body smart."

Abigail, our oldest, seems shy, but her mental wheels are constantly turning. She's processing, analyzing, and especially, planning. She's "logic smart"! The night of the November 2015 Paris terrorist attacks, she was particularly quiet and introspective. Long after we thought she was asleep, she emerged from her room having used her "word smart" to write a poem about the tragedy and victims. We had no idea how much the events of the day had troubled her. She's "self-smart."

These understandings don't just help me when I'm on the road with our girls. They've helped especially my wife homeschool them more efficiently and effectively. We can also direct them to things they'll enjoy during free time and redirect their behavior when we recognize the smarts trapping them in disobedience.

I've long loved the essay *The Weight of Glory* by C. S. Lewis, primarily for this line: "There are no ordinary people. You've never talked to a mere mortal . . . it is immortals whom we joke with, work with, marry, snub, and exploit—immortal horrors or everlasting splendours." I don't know a better description of what theologians call *imago dei* (the image of God). And yet, putting flesh on this foundational idea of the Christian faith—that every person's primary identity is being an image bearer of God Himself—is elusive. We *know* our kids are made in the image of God, but what does that *mean*?

In the opening chapters of Genesis, we read that God intended His image bearers to rule creation in a loving, productive way. In other words, humans are to be stewards of God's world. Each of the intelligences, or "smarts," that Kathy identifies in this book is a different God-given way of stewarding the world. Our job is to understand and cultivate them, in ourselves and our children.

Though our abilities and motivation to steward the world have been frustrated because of the sin of our first parents, our calling remains. Confessing our sin and acknowledging our brokenness does not deny the unique ways God created us to steward His world. Rather, in Christ's redemption we are called back to our God-given humanity, including our God-given "smarts."

So, like I've done numerous times since first learning about the multiple "smarts" from Kathy, I am recommending her book—this time to you. Jump in and learn more about your kids, and along the way, your spouse, your friends, and yourself. I'm willing to bet (because I am "logic smart" and have already thought it through) that you will be thankful you did.

JOHN STONESTREET
President, Colson Center for Christian Worldview, cohost of *BreakPoint*

"HOW AM I SMART?"
AN INTRODUCTION TO THE
EIGHT GREAT SMARTS

"Let's go!!"

"Girls, we don't want to be late."

"Mom, it's time to go again."

B etween piano and dance recitals, the local homeschool group's spring musical, a voice recital by Abbie, and all the rehearsals, Tina and her two girls, Rachel, twelve, and Abbie, thirteen, were often flying in and out of the house. Tina was glad to support them, but she sure felt like a chauffeur.

It's no surprise both girls are active in these endeavors. Intelligences awakened when children are young are more likely to develop into strengths and that's exactly what happened. Their music-smart and body-smart abilities were awakened early because their parents are musically inclined and made sure to include these kinds of activities. Their picture-smart abilities were awakened, too, which helped them imagine and embrace their roles in the musical.

God used videos of quality musicals to awaken at least three of Abbie's and Rachel's eight intelligences (or "smarts")—their music smart, picture smart, and body smart—when the girls were just preschoolers. Tina, their dad, Jeff, and I joked that the girls could have won a trivia game about Disney princesses and the Barbie videos, if anyone created such a game. They watched the videos over and over, memorized some of the dialogue, and often pretended they were Cinderella or Ariel.

Many of the videos the girls watched included gorgeous classical music recorded by some of the best orchestras in the world. At a very young age, they heard numerous instruments in stunning combinations and their music smarts were awakened.

These fast-moving productions stimulated Abbie's and Rachel's creativity and imaginations, and sparked their picture smarts. They observed characters dancing in the videos, so they danced. From twirling and leaping, they gained balance and an understanding of how their bodies work. This movement activated their body smarts.

There's more, though. Jeff and Tina's parenting didn't stop there. Because they responded to the girls' obvious interests in dance and music, their smarts weren't merely awakened. They were strengthened and, more significantly, trained.

Tina and Jeff chóse to enroll the girls in a dance class. That wise decision honored the girls' strong interest in ballet, which stemmed from their video viewing. They've now taken lessons for eight straight years.

I was privileged to attend their first dance recital. They looked adorable in their bright lime tutus with puffy velvet sleeves. Just like the other girls in the group, they stared at the audience during part of the dance, looked at the girls next to them for a while, and then managed to dance a few steps. They were perfect for young beginners.

Be sure to expose your young children to a variety of activities so their God-given passions can be awakened.

Some teen performers at the recital had clearly chosen to focus on dance. Their body smarts and music smarts were focused and trained. One dancer, in particular, impressed me. I believe she had more music-smart abilities than the other dancers. Though the other girls danced to the beat, I sensed she actually *felt* the music. She interpreted the emotion in the songs through her facial expressions and the flow of her arms. This was a beautiful example of how our eight intelligences work together. They rarely, if ever, work alone. Her music-smartness enhanced the way she used her body-smart abilities. Now Abbie and Rachel are able to do this, too.

Are your children into soccer, video games, math, or reading?

Take note of what interests them most. Be sure to expose your young children to a variety of activities so their own unique, God-designed passions can be awakened. Thoughtful parents nurture their children's development.

WHAT ARE THE MULTIPLE INTELLIGENCES?

Before knowing about multiple intelligences, I would have written the previous section about two girls who were creative and musical. I would have called them talented. I'm grateful for Dr. Howard Gardner's research and the beautiful reality that Rachel and Abbie are creative, musical, and talented *because they are smart*.

What's the big deal? Smart is a power word. Everyone wants to be smart. As I'll write about in later chapters, if some children believe others are smart and they're not, they can give up. They lower their expectations for today and tomorrow. They may not accomplish what God intended them to. This is also true of adults. Language is powerful. Words matter.

I love the freedom of thinking about children and adults through the grid of multiple intelligences. When I taught second graders, it was painful for me to realize some children were already classifying themselves as either "smart" or "not smart." Their parents were doing the classifying, too, which is probably where their children picked it up. I would have loved having the language of intelligences. I could have pointed out how Paul, Tracy, Worthy, and others were smart. This would have framed relationships, academics, our year, and their future differently.

I've met many adults who didn't have the opportunity for much post high school education. My mom was one of these, although she was extremely bright. She doubted it, at least somewhat, because she didn't have the traditional proof. She always enjoyed hearing me teach on this topic and I think that's one of the reasons.

My mom could remember significant details from the news and analyze them carefully. She co-led several very successful political campaigns for her father. She sang in tune and had a great appreciation for classical music. She had two green thumbs and made our home beautiful. She wrote and spelled well and served on various committees because of these abilities. She was a trusted friend to many and could work a room of complete strangers as well as her father, the gifted politician. *My mom was smart.* Multiple intelligences allow us to look beyond old "proofs" of grades and degrees to see evidence of smarts in life.

Although it was probably fifteen years ago, I still remember the woman who came up to me at the end of a seminar for educators. She was clearly excited so I knew her noticeable tears were tears of joy. She introduced herself as a teacher's aide and explained she had never finished her teaching degree because she hadn't thought she was smart enough. She declared, "I'm enrolling to finish immediately! I *am* smart!"

I am so privileged! It's never too late to discover more about yourself. I truly hope there are truths on these pages that bless you as a woman or man and then also as a parent, grandparent, teacher, or someone who cares about children. There is power here! Let's get more specific.

The father of the theory of multiple intelligences is Dr. Howard Gardner, of Harvard University. His first book on this topic was published in 1983. Dr. Tom Armstrong, his former colleague, has written more popularized and less academic versions of Dr. Gardner's work. I'll be using his labels for the intelligences:

THE EIGHT INTELLIGENCES		
Dr. Armstrong's Labels	*Dr. Gardner's Labels*	*Think With*
Word smart	Linguistic intelligence	Words
Logic smart	Logical-Mathematical intelligence	Questions
Picture smart	Spatial intelligence	Pictures
Music smart	Musical intelligence	Rhythm/melodies
Body smart	Bodily-Kinesthetic intelligence	Movement/touch
Nature smart	Naturalist intelligence	Patterns
People smart	Interpersonal intelligence	People
Self-smart	Intrapersonal intelligence	Reflection

If you're familiar with the theory that some people are right-brained and some are left-brained, many scholars no longer believe this theory explains as many differences among people as once thought.[1] Many of us see the theory of multiple intelligences as a much more accurate understanding of different ways people learn and process ideas.

Nature and Nurture

Dr. Gardner determined that everyone is born with each of these distinct intelligences.[2] They have to be awakened, but they're there, built into each person at birth. God uses our *nature* (our genetic makeup) and *nurture* (experiences we have and attitudes surrounding us) to create us as He wants us to be. Dr. Gardner stated the idea this way: "I reject the 'inherited versus learned' dichotomy and instead stress the interaction, from the moment of conception, between genetic and environmental factors."[3]

When "sitting at the potter's wheel" (Isaiah 64:8) and "knitting us together in our mother's womb" (Psalm 139:13–14), God chose our unique combination of genes to develop His gift of multiple intelligences. He did this for you and each of your children. He chose which smarts would be strengths. He chose you as the parent. The nurture you provide matters.

If a child grows up with apathetic or absent parents, poverty, abuse, or any number of other negative factors, his or her smarts may remain weaker throughout life. This may be partly due to lies children believe about themselves when parented in these situations. *"I don't matter." "I'll never amount to anything." "My ideas aren't important."* A child believing these truths won't bother investing in himself to develop latent gifts. The quality of your nurture matters.

Sadly, some children's intelligences don't fully develop. Perhaps illness or disease is the cause. For example, Merry, the adult daughter of a friend, is severely disabled both physically and mentally, with capabilities similar to a two-month-old. Yet Miki beams when sharing evidence that Merry's strongest intelligences are music and people. The nurturing Merry receives makes the difference. Though her development is very limited, Merry responds to music and people around her. For instance, when a prospective nurse arrives, Merry's parents have learned to use Merry's quick evaluation when determining whether to hire her. Merry will give her mom a certain look if she doesn't like the nurse, and Miki knows not to hire her.

Nature and nurture together determine which intelligences will interest your child. That's where strengths always start—with interest. Some smarts will become strengths, some may not develop much at all, and some will plateau at a point in between. When you exhibit healthy and positive attitudes and provide a variety of interesting experiences for your child, you cooperate with God in the development of his or her smarts and full potential. The nurture you provide is very important!

Awakening Smarts

Abbie and Rachel provide evidence that awakening children's smarts early is advantageous. They're more likely to become strengths. This is why the girls are still dancing and playing the piano. There are many ways to awaken the smarts. You can explore the unknown with your son, create new experiences for your daughter, and attend cultural events with your extended family.

It's never too late to awaken a part of the mind. And, it stays awake to our influence for many years. Here's what I wrote about our 100 billion neurons, the cells that are the brain's conduits of information, in *Screens and Teens: Connecting with Our Kids in a Wireless World*:

> Only about 20 percent of those connections are hard-wired by God.[4] They account for things we all learn . . . Connections of the other 80 percent of the brain's neurons are formed by what we do prior to age twenty-five.[5] Doing something a few times won't result in a firm connection, but repetitive beliefs, attitudes, and actions result in solid connections. They are considered "soft" in comparison to the hardwiring God causes during conception, but they become "harder" the more we use them. I'm thankful we can still learn new things as we age![6]

Are you encouraged? You should be! Through age twenty-five, many changes to the brain can occur. And, even after that, we can keep learning. Yes!

So, a particular intelligence might not become a definite strength because of a late start, but any smart can be improved, focused, and trained. They can also be paralyzed. I'll explain this in chapter 2.

Even though our smarts always work together, as in the example of Rachel and Abbie dancing with both their music-smart and body-smart abilities, for the purposes of this book, I'll be writing about "nature-smart children" and "people-smart children," etc. This doesn't mean these children don't have the other intelligences. It's just that I need to isolate the qualities of each in order for you to understand them.

Growth Remains

There's more. Can you picture two balloons—one that's been blown up and deflated and one that's never been used? You can tell which is which, can't you? Once stretched, a balloon never goes back to its original size. The mind is the same. Things you did when you were young stretched parts of your mind and each part will be forever larger than they were. These increases are a significant reason to provide your child with a variety of experiences during all ages and stages.

Like me. I'm a former viola player. Although I haven't played for more than thirty years, if we both picked up a viola and you've never played one, I could play better than you. Experiences awaken and then expand our smarts. That's why I could also learn to play the violin faster and more easily than someone who has never played a string instrument. Once a smart is awakened, any use of it is easier. Be encouraged!

HOW CAN UNDERSTANDING MULTIPLE INTELLIGENCES HELP CHILDREN?

There are many wonderful benefits of understanding the eight great smarts. Are you curious? Read on!

Confidence Increases

Every child wants to be smart. When your son wonders if he is or concludes that he's not, he can be defeated before starting on an assignment or listening to a teacher or you. Is your daughter ever discouraged because she doesn't think she's as smart as she thinks she needs to be? Perhaps you're sometimes disheartened, too. It's not fun!

At the beginning of my programs about our smarts, some children have a hard time believing they have all eight. Maybe school is hard for them. Or they may have been told they're stupid. Maybe they don't earn many As or Bs.

As children hear each of the intelligences described, they begin to believe the evidence I provide. They elbow their siblings or parents and I see them mouth the words, "That's me!" Their smiles, and those on parents' faces, too, indicate past hurts and current doubts are being healed and erased. Fabulous! The children relax before my eyes. By the end of the program, when I ask them to raise their hands to indicate their top four smarts, many struggle with the limit. What joy to see them go from not thinking they're smart to struggling to choose only four intelligence strengths an hour later! (It's common for parents to indicate they feel smarter, too. Yes! They'll parent better because of new understandings about their past and increased confidence. Although your child will be the focus as you continue reading, be open to discovering truths about how you are smart. Get ready to reject lies!)

When you and your child understand there are eight intelligences, the question changes from "Am I smart?" and "How smart am I?" to the much more valuable "*How* am I smart?" It's no longer about the amount of intelligence but instead about which intelligences are strengths. And, it's not as much about comparing with others as it is becoming who we were designed to be.

Children taught about the eight great smarts will apply themselves, have the confidence to tackle more challenging work, and learn more efficiently and strategically. Teach them truths from this book, talk about the smarts as situations present themselves, point out everyday uses, and affirm them specifically with language that builds them up. *"You sight-read that well because you're music smart"* is much more valuable than, *"Good job." "You're self-smart. That's why you came up with those unique ideas on your own. I'm impressed!"* is much more valuable than *"I never would have thought of that!"* or *"What made you think of that crazy idea?"*

If you're homeschooling your child, you can use many ideas in chapters 3 to 10 to teach to all eight parts of the mind. You can teach with one smart and reteach or review with another. If you're not your child's teacher, you can use different intelligences when helping your child complete homework, study for tests, and learn Scripture. Studying with more than one intelligence helps children better understand what they're learning. They'll remember what they learn longer, apply their learning more accurately, and be more optimistic for the future. Their grades will often improve.

Less Likely to Believe They're Dumb

Children are empowered when they're taught about the eight ways they are smart. They learn they have some smarts that are strengths and some that aren't. The new question, *"How* am I smart?" is a key. This is very different from believing intelligence is limited and they don't have enough.

Children can learn to discern which smarts to rely on during different academic and social activities. This gives them some control over how they do, builds confidence, and increases effort. Intelligence isn't fixed and it's not narrow. It's very wide and all-encompassing. God was generous when He created us as He did!

When something is hard for children who know they're smart in many ways, they can think about whether using a different intelligence would help. When they don't do well on an assignment or test, they know they can approach the content differently by studying with a different smart. Their default won't be to believe, "I'm dumb." Rather, they'll think, "I can improve by using another smart." (As I'll share in the next chapter, it's also essential that they understand how important their character is. Using the most relevant smarts *and* the most relevant character qualities is essential.)

Parents who only tell their children they're smart, and don't also talk about the role of character, create a dangerous situation.

Children who don't know they have multiple intelligences will often feel dumb when they get a "bad" grade and when tasks are challenging. They have nothing else to rely on. They believe their intelligence is fixed and causes all outcomes—those that turn out well and those that don't.

Parents who only tell their children they're smart, and don't also talk about the role of character, create a dangerous situation.[7] Now, if their children don't do well, they can only blame their lack of intelligence. This can quickly result in hopelessness. They may then slide down a slippery slope to apathy, self-rejection, and lowered expectations. These children may never accomplish what God designed them to do.

A New Way to Talk about Behavior

Teaching children to ask an additional question, "How can I be smart with my smarts?" introduces the powerful idea that children can use their smarts in healthy *or* unhealthy ways. Children who understand that their positive and negative behaviors are often related to different smarts have new ways of thinking about obedience. Parents have new ways of motivating excellent behavior and talking with their children about why they misbehave. (See chapter 2 for a full presentation of this concept.)

Volunteering and Career Choice

How a child is smart can also direct decisions regarding volunteering and serving. For example, a child who is nature smart and people smart may enjoy helping out at a pet shelter. One who is nature smart and body smart may enjoy walking a neighbor's dog. Many examples are included in chapters 3 to 10 so you'll understand how these smarts work together. Keep reading!

Careers can also be identified as a good fit or not according to a child's smarts. My nephew, Andy, who played with Legos and toy trains much longer than other boys might have, did so because he is very picture smart and logic smart. He is now a successful engineer using those skills and his people-smart abilities. He consults with many customers so his people-smart skills are essential. Remember, intelligences never work alone. They support each other.

Five Core Needs Can Be Met

Another advantage the smarts provide is an important way for children to meet their legitimate, core needs. This means they'll be less likely to rely on counterfeit hope and dangerous ways of trying to meet their needs—lying, teasing, pride, apathy, popularity, and more.

When needs are met, it's more likely your child will experience contentment, peace, excellence, fulfillment, obedience, and much more. Knowing which intelligences are strengths and how to use them in smart ways can help your child meet these five basic needs.[8]

Security: Who can I trust?

Children who know *how* they are smart can have more security in themselves. They'll believe they can do well and will be more confident even when by themselves in new circumstances. They'll also have healthy security in you when you're the one who teaches them how they are smart and how to be smart with their smarts. They will trustingly turn to you for help and believe you when you speak into their lives.

Honestly, because God designed us with these needs, we're healthiest when He meets them. Related to security, when presenting the smarts to children in a Christian context, I include this reality: *"God is smarter than I am!"* They laugh and sometimes cheer. Smart children understand that God will always be smarter than they are. In addition, smart children know they need the smartest God—the God of the Bible. I tell them that God could have created them to be like marionette puppets He controls. Instead, He gave them eight different intelligences and He trusts them to use their smarts to help and not hurt. That's humbling, isn't it?

The smarts are great, but they're no substitute for God. None! Our smarts are extremely important and I know many who have improved lives and perspectives concerning their futures because of what they learned about multiple intelligences. I hope this will include you. But these understandings won't lead to the rock-solid foundation and fulfillment only God can provide.

I hear about children with negative labels finding each other and having a party in the corner.

Identity: Who am I?

Identity needs to be current, honest, and complete. Children need to know their strengths and challenges. Knowing about multiple intelligences spins what they may have known about themselves in a positive light. For example, rather than thinking, *"Spelling is hard because I'm really stupid!*" they'll understand "*Spelling is hard because I'm logic smart and not very picture smart.*" Discovering how they are smart also reveals many new and reliable truths. Because identity controls behavior, it's important for children to know who they are.

As I've already written, children who know *how* they are smart will apply themselves more regularly and respond to challenges more optimistically. Thinking they're smart isn't enough. It's knowing *how* they are smart that empowers their identity.

Belonging: Who wants me?

Children's belonging is dependent upon the quality of their security and identity. When one or both of these needs aren't met or they're met in unhealthy ways, children either won't experience belonging at all or their belonging will be unhealthy. Picture this: Children who believe they're dumb will hang out with peers who believe the same thing about themselves. Many teachers have told me that's exactly what happens. I hear about children with negative labels finding each other and having a party in the corner. Seriously!

When children know *how* they are smart, they can discern who is smart in the same ways. They can get to know them and have things in common to talk about and dreams for their tomorrows to share. When working on projects and needing help, they can recognize who has smart strengths they don't have that they'd benefit from. They can choose to go for a walk in the park when dating someone who is nature smart, visit an art museum with someone who is picture smart, and expect deep conversations with someone who is self-smart. Knowing about the smarts can strengthen relationships.

Purpose: Why am I alive?

The core needs continue to build upon each other. Therefore, children's purpose will be healthiest when their security is strong. They need to know their strengths to believe they have purpose. Children who know *how* they are smart as part of their identity are typically more optimistic about the future. When their belonging is strong, they'll have people to serve and people to serve with. These people compel children to discover and fulfill their purpose.

Children listen intently when I get to talk with them about how they've all been created on purpose to leave the world a better place. Examples of how they can do this according to their combination of smarts always enthuses them. When you share ideas with children, you expand their horizons and awaken and confirm their passions.

As you continue reading, you'll see children in a new light. For example, nature-smart children will more readily volunteer to weed their grandparents' garden than other children. Logic-smart children will enjoy teaching a friend or sibling about a new math app. Children who are word smart, logic smart, and people smart may want to become ethical journalists who don't let their biases influence their reporting. If they're body smart and picture smart, they may want to create beautiful sculptures that glorify God and reveal their God-given abilities.

Competence: What do I do well?

The core needs culminate with competence. Many parents think what children do well is most important. It's the need that garners the most concern, energy, and conversations. But guess what? Without healthy ways to meet the first four needs, it's rare children will have competence. They think they don't need it if they don't have purpose and people to serve. If their identity is only negative and they have no one to trust, including themselves, they won't believe they can do anything well. You must pay attention to how the first four needs are met—multiple intelligences help in many ways. That's part of the power of multiple intelligences. They offer great explanatory power for the important things of life.

Children who know *how* they are smart will be resourceful and effectively achieve more. Knowing their strengths, they'll want to use them. For instance, what they do well will influence what they choose to do in their spare time, courses they take, subjects they choose to study on their own, and more. They'll find workarounds when they're challenged—making a hard task easier by using one of their smart strengths that others might not see as relevant.

The hope I see in children's eyes when I teach them the smarts is largely because they discover how relevant these are to their whole lives. Their joy and success. Overcoming challenges. School, church, friends, family, present, future. With their new understandings, they're empowered to more successfully meet all five core needs in positive ways. Excellent!

HOW CAN I IDENTIFY MY CHILD'S MULTIPLE INTELLIGENCE STRENGTHS?

Your child's smarts will usually be apparent first as interests. Therefore, spending time with your children—to see them and to hear them—is essential. When you and others notice their interests and nurture them by your positive responses, abilities will usually emerge and be strengthened. So, look for interests first. What does your son do in his spare time? What does your daughter spend her gift money on? What does your son keep talking about after school? Pay attention and ask yourself which smarts are represented. As you continue to be alert, you'll discover whether these were fleeting interests or whether they give birth to real strengths.

As I'll elaborate on in chapter 2, and include in each remaining chapter, paying attention to how each child misbehaves can also reveal smart strengths. Do they talk too much? Word smart.

Move more than is appropriate and touch everything? Body smart. Manipulate people—even you? People smart. Think they must have reasons for everything before they obey? Logic smart. You get the idea.

School subjects and topics aligned with strong intelligences will usually be easiest and more enjoyable for your child so this is another thing to pay attention to. For example, history, fiction, and creative writing are related to being picture smart. Science is aligned with being logic smart and/or nature smart. Drama is often related to being people smart.

Teaching your child about the smarts can also help you identify intelligence strengths and weaknesses. You can observe reactions to details and examples you share and note which ones pique his or her curiosity. Then ask *your child* to identify his or her strengths. Your child will often know and be able to provide evidence. Your child may also be able to indicate which of the smarts are weak. (As you'll understand after reading chapter 10, children who are not very self-smart will have a harder time with this self-analysis.)

It's easier to identify strengths for older children. When children are young, because smarts are being awakened, their interests vary. They may build with blocks for a solid week and then want to investigate everything outside. They may discover a toy that makes noise and now be very interested in music. As children age, the top several smarts will usually become obvious. In the meantime, keep using them all.

Don't do this so they all become strengths or "top smarts." As I've already written, that's not realistic. And don't try to develop them or use them all at the same time. That's overwhelming. I know too many children who need their own appointment calendars because they're so busy. That's not healthy. As you'll come to understand as you read more, aim to expose your children to all the smarts as opportunities arise and strengths will naturally reveal themselves as you parent with balance.

Awakening, strengthening, and training children's multiple intelligences are key ways to help them become who God created them uniquely to be. Nurture their smarts and discern which are passions and potentials. This means you will also discern which will remain less important to your children. Work to accept God's choices for them. Your attitudes are essential to helping your children fulfill their God-given niche in the family, community, church, and in history. This is a significant responsibility!

To help you evaluate your child's smarts so you can better meet his or her needs, we've created a website where you can complete checklists about the smarts. Your child can do it, too, so you can compare your ratings, which should generate beneficial conversations. The website is www.8GreatSmarts.com and your password is AHA3374.

"I WILL BE SMART WITH MY SMARTS!"
MULTIPLE INTELLIGENCES AND CHARACTER INTERSECT

"She's such a Chatty Kathy."

Grandma Meier was the first to bestow this nickname upon me when I was about two and a half years old. I was quite a talker so the label fit.

Now I earn a living talking and writing. Let that sink in a bit. I talked because it was natural and normal. Now I talk on purpose. It's still natural.

My intelligence strengths were noticed early and called out of me in positive ways. You can do the same for your child. That's part of your nurturing power as a parent. Specifically, my word-smart strengths had a lot to do with my joy and success as a child. They were acknowledged and celebrated by my family and teachers.

They also had much to do with the dreams I dreamt for my future and the fulfilling life I now live. This book wouldn't exist had my parents not valued my abilities and raised me to use them well.

My brother, Dave, and I were encouraged to read and our parents often read to us. I have memories of our dad reading books on his own, but I don't of our mom. Throughout her adult years, she didn't enjoy reading books in her spare time. She would flip through magazines and devour the newspaper, though, as did our dad. Dave and I still read "old-fashioned" newspapers today.

Teachers matter— and this includes homeschool parents who get to know their children especially well.

As my mom demonstrates, you don't have to enjoy or be good at something in order for your kids to embrace it. It helps, but it's not essential. My mom's attitudes toward my reading and education in general were more important than whether she read or not. Because my love of reading was nurtured, I won a summer reading contest at the library when I was an elementary school student. I chose *Little Women* as one of my awards. I still have the book with the certificate inside. My parents were proud of me and I was affirmed. Positive attitudes might be some of the best nurturing you provide.

I wasn't only nurtured in the area of reading. When I was about ten, my parents enrolled me in children's theater. I joke now that they said, "Go talk there awhile." I actually don't remember how they spun it, but I know it wasn't about me using up my words there so I'd come home and be quiet. My talking was affirmed. It was about my enjoyment and discovering a positive and purposeful use for my natural ability. It was also about meeting other children with similar talents and interests. Parents matter.

The high school forensics team was another relevant outlet for me. I valued words and was beginning to experience more of their power and nuances. Talking to inform or persuade as a part of a team earning ribbons was fun and challenging. My choice to participate was partially birthed in classes and discussions with my English teacher. Teachers matter—and this includes homeschool parents who get to know their children especially well.

Strengths not harnessed can become weaknesses.

Watching my grandpa Meier give numerous speeches when I was young also motivated my involvement. He served as mayor of our city when I was in elementary school and junior high. He used words only to help people and not to hurt; only for good and not to do harm. His example remains a strong motivation for me today. What I watched him do, I want to do well. Family matters.

Why am I including all of this in a chapter about character? Because strengths not harnessed can become weaknesses. Too much of a good thing isn't always a good thing. For instance, those of us with word-smart strengths can gossip well, tease well, impress with our vocabulary, and always want to have the last word. I tell children that just because we can do it doesn't mean we should. I know I didn't always use my smarts well. If my parents wouldn't have affirmed my healthy uses of my abilities and provided positive outlets for them, I might have gravitated more toward the negative. That would have been sad. More importantly, it might have meant I wouldn't have developed the strengths God chose for me (Ephesians 2:10).

Not Being Smart with Your Smarts

Word-smart children aren't the only ones who can use their smarts in unhealthy ways. Since picture-smart children like drawing and creating, they might color on the report you wrote for your boss and left on the table. Logic-smart children like exploring things on their own, so they might walk away from you during a family field trip to go investigate something that catches their attention. Body-smart children may touch everything in a museum and music-smart children may make noise constantly.

It's not okay if children are misbehaving because of how they are smart. We can't excuse their choices because they have talent and ability. Identifying the smart giving birth to misbehavior helps you talk with your children wisely. When children understand the cause of their behavior, they are more empowered to change. You'll have more hope, too!

One of my coworkers heard me speak on this topic. As we talked on the drive back from the training event, she began to see her ten-year-old grandson in a new and very positive light. She realized the behaviors that often irritated his classmates were rooted in his body-smart and logic-smart strengths. That night, she lovingly explained to him what she had learned and asked if he agreed with her that he was very body smart and logic smart. He lit up when discovering he was smart in these two important ways. My coworker told me later that her grandson was different that morning. Her summary comment says a lot: "It makes a difference to be understood, doesn't it?" Yes!

During programs for children, I demonstrate that much of the trouble they get into is a result of using their strengths in the wrong ways or at the wrong times. They laugh and that's fine. Then they get serious. That's better. I teach them they can choose to be dumb, but God didn't make them that way. Being smart is a choice. So is stupidity. Children can choose to *not* use their intelligences, to let their strengths get them into trouble, or to use their smarts for harmful purposes.

Children are not necessarily stupid and not necessarily bad. Maybe they just haven't learned self-respect, self-control, and respect for others. These are keys to children (and adults) being able to use their intelligence strengths for good and not evil, to help and not hurt.

Does your son keep his eyes glued to his book when you ask him to help with the dishes? He may be *word smart*. Does your daughter struggle with obedience because she's always asking, "Why?" She may be *logic smart*. Does your daughter doodle all over her notes rather than studying her notes? She may be *picture smart*. Does your son irritate others with his constant humming and finger tapping? He may be *music smart*. Do your children constantly move and touch everything? They may be *body smart*. Does your daughter pay so much attention to her cats that she doesn't finish her homework? She may be *nature smart*. Does your son interrupt you constantly because he needs to know what you think about his ideas? He may be *people smart*. Does your daughter get lost in her thoughts and ignore your input? She may be *self-smart*.

Paralyzing Smarts: The Impact of Criticism

Can you imagine what might have happened if my parents and teachers had seen my word-smart abilities as irritating problems to eliminate rather than as strengths to develop, focus, and train? What might have happened if I had been raised hearing, "*Be quiet . . . shut up . . . go find something to do . . . I'm sick of your talking!*" Would I be a speaker and author? No. My strengths might have been paralyzed, so I wouldn't use them at all, or I might have used them only in unhealthy ways because of the negative environment in which I was raised.

Rather, my parents, brother, grandparents, and others listened to me. We listened to each other. We had rich give-and-take conversations at the dinner table. My brother, Dave, and I weren't raised to be quiet unless spoken to. We were encouraged to speak up. We were also taught to listen and to respect whoever was speaking.

We weren't "told." We were "taught."

Was I sometimes asked to be quiet? Absolutely! Did I sometimes need to leave my brother, parents, and friends alone? Absolutely! Did I sometimes need to listen to my brother? Yes! I'm thankful that he and I were raised to respect ourselves and others and to develop and use our self-control.

Without even realizing what they were doing, our parents demonstrated strong, purposeful, and healthy uses of the smarts. They challenged Dave and me to be smart with our smarts, taught us how to do that, and provided new guidance when we weren't. The key word for me there is "taught." We weren't "told." We were "taught." And, we were corrected and retaught. Negative consequences were implemented when we didn't comply. Positive ones were used when we were smart with our smarts.

Paralysis often occurs when children use their smarts in unhealthy ways. Disobedience can often draw a look that paralyzes. Most parents know *that* look and kids demonstrate it for me when I ask. Believe me, it's not hard! Tone of voice can also paralyze smarts. It doesn't always, of course, but if it's consistently negative or angry, children might stop using the smart they believe is causing the critical reactions. The same is true for what is said and what is not said. What might your children be waiting to hear? What have they heard often enough?

In general, criticism paralyzes intelligences. This includes criticism of finished projects and criticism of processes used (handwriting, the way books and papers are organized, and talking with friends rather than working alone). Specific correction is appropriate. Criticism isn't.[1] I'll never forget the young boy who told me he enjoyed playing the piano and thought he was doing well one particular day until his dad angrily shouted from another room, *Stop all that racket in there!* He told me he instantly lifted his hands from the keys and begged his mom to let him stop taking lessons.

Regular punishment of strengths (movement for body-smart children, talking for word-smart children, and exploring for logic-smart children) can also paralyze the associated smarts so children no longer use them.

Teasing can also paralyze smarts. It doesn't matter who does the teasing. It hurts and plants seeds of doubt. This is also true when out-of-the-box thinking isn't well received. If children often hear, "That would never work" and "We've never done it that way!" they may eventually stop thinking altogether.

Paralysis can also set in due to weaknesses. For example, a

student who reads orally in a choppy and slow manner may know the teacher is disappointed and frustrated. This may cause him or her to avoid reading aloud again. Discouragement may set in for children who struggle to creatively write well who don't have their work displayed on bulletin boards like most classmates.

A girl waited in line with others after my program. She fidgeted while waiting her turn. When she made it to the front of the line, she looked up with the saddest face. "My mommy didn't know what my picture was. My teacher loved it and put it on the special wall, but my mommy didn't even know what it was. She kind of scrunched her face and asked 'What is that?' in that kind of weird way that made me think she didn't really like it. It was a giraffe and she didn't even know." Her voice trailed off . . .

Race and gender biases can also paralyze.

Perfectionism often shuts down smarts because it doesn't allow children any freedom to explore and grow. Your child knows mistakes will most likely occur when trying new things. If your daughter thinks she needs to be perfect, she won't risk trying something new. Was this girl's mom expecting her to paint a perfect giraffe? Was that fair and realistic?

Do you often respond to your son's attempts to help around the house by exclaiming, "Just let me do it!"? This decreases his initiative and confidence and suggests he's not good enough. Paralysis sets in. If you notice your child no longer growing in a smart that had once been a strength, see if perfectionism has set in and then talk and teach against it.[2]

Race and gender biases can also paralyze. How unfortunate! For example, Randy detailed for me that his picture-smart strengths weren't affirmed by his parents when he was young. This created great confusion, frustration, and even anger.

Randy was taught that art was irrelevant and frivolous for boys. Because he was always visualizing, daydreaming, and doodling, he believed he wasn't very smart. His mom wanted him to be "the brains," so he was forced into what Randy refers to as his linear (math and accounting) phase. Randy became angry after a while, as he realized that his mom hadn't been able to recognize an innate gift and tried to instill a different one in him. He had to grieve the loss of time and seek God's understanding. I'm glad he did! When he turned thirty-five, he purchased special pens and paper and started drawing again. I own some of his drawings and they're amazing. Although paralyzed for a long, long time, his picture-smart abilities were still there. Some key conversations and encounters reawakened this smart. Thank God, it's never too late for an intelligence to awaken and be reawakened, strengthened, focused, and trained!

Reawakening Smarts

As I mentioned in chapter 1, children are born with the capacity to develop all eight smarts. They are awakened (or not) through engaging experiences. I have great news! If paralysis sets in, the right experiences can reawaken the smarts. Isn't God good to give us second and third chances? Yes!

Very few parents set out to paralyze their children's intelligences. Yet it happens. Sometimes the smart affected is shut down permanently. It will remain a weak area for the child's lifetime. In other cases, interacting with key ideas and positive people can reawaken the smart.

If you have paralyzed a child's intelligence, the paralysis can be undone if you or others create energizing experiences that follow. Although it's ideal when these quickly follow the pain of paralysis, it's never too late, as we can see from Randy's illustration. You must be aware, though, that your child may not quickly respond. This is because the paralyzing experience at least partially destroyed his or her security.

Children tell me that when we apologize, the reawakening especially begins. Were you too quickly angry with your logic-smart child, not listening to the entire question? Realize it and sincerely communicate your sorrow. Were you critical of your son's piano playing, even though he was a beginner and you wanted his music-smart ability to develop? Apologize and sit down to listen to him play so you can encourage him. Were you constantly pointing out your people-smart daughter's unwise uses of her ability and never acknowledging her occasional healthy uses?

Talk about it and apologize.

Observe carefully to recognize the depth of your child's concern so you can strategically enter into the situation. When you read fun material together orally, the pain of classmates' laughter can lift. When you ask the teacher how to help your child improve his or her writing, work together in a casual and nonthreatening way, and celebrate your child's improvements, so you can reignite your child's enjoyment of writing.

Before the young girl walked off after telling me about her painting of a giraffe, she became a bit more confident, looked me in the eye again, and declared, "I think I *am* picture smart and I am going to draw again because you told me I can. Thank you." I was stunned and deeply encouraged. As a complete stranger, I was still able to speak hope over her.

Character Qualities: Beyond the Smarts

From what you've read so far, can you predict how character qualities are relevant to multiple intelligences? Let me explain two very important categories:

Self-respect, self-control, and respect for others. When children (and adults) respect themselves, they're more able to believe in their present and future value. They're also more likely to reject lies about themselves. Therefore, it's less likely they'll develop bad habits that could result in their smarts being paralyzed due to their misbehavior and your reactions.

As children mature and understand more about their smarts, they will want them awakened, developed, focused, and trained so they can use them in valuable ways. This motivation can lead to self-control. They'll work to strengthen skills and smarts they believe they need. They'll focus on positives, use their smarts in healthy ways, and not sabotage their success.

Will your daughter believe in herself and be glad about which smarts are strengths if you're not? If she hears you constantly comparing her to someone else, she may begin to reject herself. She may try to please you by working to develop a smart that isn't strong. I've met children who, by doing this, eventually feel defeated in all smarts. Their strong smarts weaken because of lack of attention or rejection because they're trying so hard for their parents to notice and appreciate them. Jill Savage and I wrote how essential it is that parents love their children for who they are and consistently communicate acceptance in our book *No More Perfect Kids*.[3] If this is relevant for your current parenting pattern, check it out.

Perseverance, effort, initiative, diligence, teachability, thoroughness, responsibility. Character qualities like these are very relevant for all children (and adults) at all times. We need to consistently teach them to our children. They rarely come naturally. Character is relevant when intelligences aren't strong and may be most relevant when they are.

You don't want your son relying *only* on how he is smart when approaching new tasks. He could be unsure of himself that day, overwhelmed, or confused. The assignment could be a bit beyond his natural abilities. As explained in chapter 1, it's easy for children to feel dumb when they believe their smarts have failed them. Your son needs to understand that his successes and challenges are always due to how he is smart *plus* how he applies himself. Therefore, it's important to affirm the character qualities and learning processes children use that contribute to their successes.[4]

As with so many other things, our modeling of the character qualities we want our children to use is important. When we appropriately persevere, it's easier for children to persevere in our presence. They'll feel safe being vulnerable. They'll know we understand that sometimes they have to work to be successful. Of course, this is true for each of these character qualities. I tell children all the time that if they work hard, it's because they're smart. When they're teachable, they're smart. When they're responsible and take responsibility for their actions, they're smart. On and on.

Think of your own life. Did God use these and other character qualities to help you awaken or strengthen a smart or two? What about helping you overcome paralysis and reawakening the smarts? You'll read about some of my examples in the next chapters. Here are two brief illustrations to show you what I mean: I used initiative to learn to enjoy picture-smart activities with friends. This isn't a strong smart for me, but I wanted to understand it better to connect with good friends. I used teachability and respect for others when at the Powell Gardens in Kansas City with a friend who is extremely nature smart and wanted me to know more. I didn't really need to know what she wanted to teach me, but I put my friend first. What about you? I hope you're looking forward to helping your children learn how to do this.

I AM WORD SMART: I THINK WITH WORDS

"Sweetheart, Mommy's ears are full. I can't listen anymore."
"Just tip your head and make the words fall out. Then you'll have room for more."

Is your child this word smart? Talking to think. Talking during play. Talking to no one. Talking to everyone. Many moms and dads of word-smart children admit to being exhausted because their children seem to talk from morning to night. God trusts you to listen, engage in conversations when they want you to, and not paralyze them as they develop this God-given intelligence.

As with the other intelligences, there is a hierarchy of smartness. For example, your daughter may be able to communicate in more than one language. This would make her more word smart than someone who can write, read, speak, and listen well in one language. Or, perhaps your son speaks and listens well, but reading and writing have been slower to develop. But maybe he is young so it's not appropriate to think in terms of "slower." Rather, developing these skills is going to take time and experience.

As designed by God, all children have the capacity to develop this smart, but not all children will have it as one of their top strengths. Whether it will be a strength depends upon God's call on each child's life. Your preferences are relevant, too, as I'll show in upcoming chapters.

Just because you're a reader doesn't mean your kids will be.

Speaking of preferences, because word smart is one of the most important ones for academic success, you'll probably want to prioritize it. All parents want their children to do well in school. But it's more than that. The skills rooted in being word smart serve us well our whole lives.

Children and adults read textbooks, literature, books for pleasure, questions on tests, information on websites, and more. Children and adults write essays and reports, take notes during classes and seminars, complete written assignments, make to-do lists, and more. Children and adults listen to lectures, videos, instructions, comments during discussions, and more. Children and adults talk when asking questions, sharing during discussions, participating in small group work, eating lunch with friends, and more.

If your child is older and has had plenty of exposure to good books and excellent teaching and you realize that word smart is not going to be one of your child's strengths, that's okay—if you decide it's okay. If, however, it's not okay with you, your child may pick up on this. He or she may experience stress and feel unaccepted and even dumb as you continue to want him or her to achieve what is clearly out of reach.

A challenge for parents, but an absolute necessity, is to accept and love the children you have. Just because you're a reader doesn't mean your kids will be. Or maybe you're not and they are. Both scenarios have to be okay or your children will experience painful rejection. That can quickly give rise to self-rejection, including a rejection of strengths they think you don't value.

In my seminars, it's easy to hear an audible gasp when I state, "Raise the children you were given and not the ones you wish you had." Parents almost always have to set aside some dreams they had when they found out they'd be parents. Parents must grieve what isn't and accept what is.[1] It's not easy, but it is essential. Learning to trust their future to God is important.

Don't for a minute think that because a smart isn't a strength, your child can't be content or successful. Maybe with the old-fashioned view of intelligence being fixed, this might have been the case.[2] But remember what I wrote about in chapter 1. Once used, intelligences never go back to their original size. And, your child's smarts never work alone. Children can learn to use strong ones alongside weaker ones. They can tap into their character and diligently practice and strategically study to improve. They can surround themselves with healthy people who can encourage them and strengthen missing skills. You!

As I'll explain more in the next two chapters, spelling doesn't come naturally to me. Yet, I'm an author and blogger. I'm passionate about my ideas and helping parents so I find ways to cope with my spelling challenges. This deficit isn't enough to stop me from pursuing my call. Why? Because God wins and because I was parented to know more about my strengths than my weaknesses. As I tell children all the time, we can't let our weaknesses win. Would you like to chant that with me as children do in my programs? "I must not let my weaknesses win!" One more time! "I must not let my weaknesses win!"

WORD SMART:
WRITING AND TALKING AND MORE

Word-smart children think with words. When they're excited they almost always talk. They need time to read and they need to be heard when they want an audience. They get joy from using exactly the right word at the right time. Their power is language.

Although word-smart children like talking with others, they don't *need* an audience. They're often content talking to themselves while they play, work, and study. Sometimes you'll hear them, but sometimes they'll admit to talking to themselves inside their heads where no one else can hear.

During my presentations on the eight smarts, I ask children if they are distracted by their own voices—even when they are trying hard to listen to you or their teach-

Children who are very word smart may begin talking at an early age.

ers. Many of them laugh and raise their hands. It's fun for them to discover others talk inside their minds like they do.

Children who are very word smart may begin talking at an early age. They may have been more curious about writing than their siblings and learned their letters easily. When older, they write willingly and well and read in their spare time for information and/or enjoyment. They handle most textbooks and assignments successfully, often being able to remember details. They have a large vocabulary, and they speak confidently and can listen accurately. They tend to be well informed and often want to share their opinions and ideas with others. Also, learning and retaining a new language easily and using what they know is further evidence of being word smart. For all these reasons, most word-smart children enjoy school and do well there.

There are many ways these children's abilities can benefit others. They can serve on their school yearbook committee, volunteer to tutor children at a homeless shelter, assist in children's church when they're too old to attend themselves, listen attentively to their great-aunt's stories, and/or hone their speaking abilities as part of a speech team. They may also learn a second language and serve God during a summer mission trip with people who use that language.

Look for patterns of interest and ability, not isolated occurrences.

Most word-smart children are good at explaining things. They may help their sisters and brothers understand something. They may tutor peers or students younger than them. They may also argue, persuade, and entertain with words. Does this sound like one or more of your children?

If your son does not argue well, he still might be quite word smart. Arguing is rooted in word *and* logic smart. So if your son doesn't argue, it's possible that logic smart is not one of his strengths. However, word smart still could be. It's also possible that he is logic smart, but his character and Christlikeness prevent him from arguing, as they should for all of us.

A child who demonstrates most of the behaviors I included here could be classified as having word-smart strengths. In contrast, a child who talks a lot, but doesn't necessarily talk to explain or persuade, or who doesn't enjoy writing, may be an auditory learner instead of a word-smart child. This means she remembers best the things she hears herself say. It's an important strength and can help with academics, but it's not the same as being word smart. While reading these chapters, you'll want to determine whether your child has high or low interest and high or low abilities according to each smart's explanation. Look for *what* they do and *how much* of it they do. Look for *patterns* of ability and interest, not isolated occurrences.

LEARNING MATTERS:
BEING "SCHOOL SMART"

Because so much of school involves reading, writing, speaking, and listening, children with word-smart strengths will usually do very well. That's why I refer to this smart as a "school smart." It's not that it's not important outside of school. It is. But it's especially important for school.

When this one isn't in the top four smarts, school can be very challenging. It's not uncommon for these children to feel dumb. Once children decide they're not smart, they often lower their expectations for their current courses and for their future. They may not bother trying the bonus spelling words. They'll write the shortest book report allowed. They may not study because they decide it doesn't matter. *"I'm stupid. Studying won't help."* They may decide continuing their education past high school makes no sense.

Of course, these sabotaging behaviors contribute to less learning and lower grades, thus reinforcing children's opinions that they're stupid. Please watch for these types of choices and talk with your children. If this smart isn't strong, help them see the value of supporting it with other smarts that are strengths and positive behaviors rather than giving up.

If you believe you're not smart simply because reading, writing, speaking, and/or listening didn't come easily to you or you didn't enjoy school, reconsider this conclusion before going any further. I've met many adults who decided they were stupid because of how teachers treated them, what parents said about them, what parents never said, and how easily school came to a sibling. I don't have enough fingers to count the number of times I've heard, *"My brother was the smart one."*

I wish your parents and teachers would have understood you have multiple intelligences, but they didn't. I'm grateful you're learning about them now. It's not too late for you to reframe your reality. For example:

"My sister was and is more word smart than me. But that doesn't mean I'm not word smart at all."

"Word smart may not be one of my top smarts so school was challenging. But I'm not dumb and I'm looking forward to discovering which smarts are my strengths."

Strengthening Word Smart: Reading Aloud, Making Lists . . .

The same learning methods that are effective and easy for children with word-smart strengths can be used to further awaken and strengthen this smart when it's weak. It will probably take longer for a non-word-smart child to use the methods independently and efficiently. You also may want to explain the advantages of the methods so they know why to use one method over another.

One of the best ways to strengthen reading is to simply read out loud often. This is true for all ages. Choose good literature and a variety of genres, usually above your child's reading level. Read with good expression. Use nonfiction (especially if you believe logic smart may be a strength) and fiction, poetry, humor, adventure stories, biographies, and the like. Observe to see if one appears more engaging than another. Then use that one more.

When I taught second graders, I remember inspiring many children by using different versions of the same fairy tales. Children enjoyed analyzing similarities and differences, and since they were familiar with the stories, they were more confident when reading. Picture-smart children found these activities especially engaging. Their ability to enjoy and critique illustrations and discuss how they were the factor when choosing their favorite versions improved their reading interest.

Writing interest and ability can be positively affected by using real tasks. Think about how you actually use writing and model those uses. Look for opportunities for your children to use writing in similar ways. For instance, you can help your daughter write a thank-you letter to her dance teacher. Help your son make a list of things he needs before baseball practices begin. He can use this list to let his grandparents know what he could use for his birthday. He could then send them a short email about this.

It's also effective to use many different writing materials. For example, the very children who say they can't write their spelling sentences might write detailed and accurate ones when getting to choose gel pens and colored paper. (As you'll come to understand when reading chapter 5, this will be especially true if they have picture-smart abilities.)

Speaking and listening can also be improved with a variety of experiences. Using authentic tasks strategically can help more than isolated practice. It can be as simple as watching short informational videos together on topics your child is interested in and then talking about what you heard. Encourage your child to ask and answer questions and to share ideas learned elsewhere. You can do the same thing by just observing what you notice when out-and-about running errands.

Learning Struggles: What if It Comes Too Easy?

Even though word-smart skills are a key to school success, children with this strength can still run into academic challenges. It usually has to do with which other smarts are strengths and which are weaker. This will make more sense when you've read more of the book and learned how the other smarts operate. But let me give you some examples that I think you'll understand.

Even though I'm very word smart, reading fiction isn't as easy for me as reading nonfiction. Because I'm also logic smart, reading for information is more engaging for me. Add to this the reality that I'm not very picture smart. I don't naturally see in pictures with my eyes. I don't see the action in my mind so I don't necessarily enjoy it or remember it. Perhaps you can relate. Or, maybe like friends of mine, you can't relate at all!

For similar reasons, creative writing isn't easy for me. Adding adjectives and action verbs to my writing doesn't come naturally. I have to remember to do it because I don't think with my eyes. I might be satisfied writing, "The ball bounced." But people who read what I write want to read, "The blue, underinflated ball bounced erratically down the winding staircase."

Please don't let my mention of smarts you haven't read about yet overwhelm you. The smarts never work alone and I want you to begin thinking about this important truth here at the very beginning. As you keep reading, I'll refer to combinations and you'll think of some, too. We can almost always help children with a weak smart by showing them how to use a stronger smart at the same time. And, strong smarts can explain why some things are challenging. Ultimately, I believe you'll find it all very encouraging. (You might want to remember the chart in chapter 1 on page 18 since what each smart thinks with is listed there.)

What if I suggested that word-smart children can struggle

academically due to a lack of character, as I wrote about in chapter 2? Follow this reasoning: Learning tends to come easily to word-smart children. At first, they don't need to persevere or practice much. They just rely on their ability. Then, there may be a challenging assignment, a confusing lecture, or a topic that doesn't interest them. They struggle. These students can panic at the thought of not being bright anymore. The longer we allow them to think success is only a matter of the mind and character is irrelevant, the greater the likelihood they may struggle at some point. Agree?

If your child has word-smart strengths, affirm them and celebrate them. But also talk about their character *from the very beginning*. Don't allow them to think it's irrelevant. Affirm them for being self-motivated. For caring about doing their best. For being interested and teachable. For following through and finishing on time. For not procrastinating.

Teaching the Word-Smart Child: Building a "Listening Vocabulary"

When studying and learning with this smart, your child can read, write, and speak about a topic. Word-smart children enjoy listening to others talk about it, recopying or typing lecture notes, and reading other books about the topic, even if the books weren't assigned.

Various teaching methods will be effective with word-smart children, including storytelling, lectures, discussions, putting words on the board during lectures, note-taking strategies, word games, choral reading, journal writing, drawing upon a variety of books and literary genres, using audiobooks, and writing research reports and other kinds of assignments. They may be equally comfortable reading and writing with devices and paper.[3]

Especially when word-smart children also have strengths in logic, debate works, too. This is a positive use of the same skills that often make arguing easy for these children. With people-smart strengths, they can more easily give persuasive speeches than others. And, if they're picture smart, they can illustrate stories they write.

Make it a priority to read to children and engage them in meaningful conversations, because these activities increase children's listening vocabulary. These are the words children understand when they hear them even if they can't read or spell them. Because listening vocabulary is one of the best predictors of school success, it's crucial to develop it in every child.

WHEN THEY GROW UP: CAREERS AND EDUCATION

The same things that cause school and learning to be easy or hard are relevant to think about when wondering what careers will be a good fit. This includes the decision about whether more than a high school education is necessary or preferred.

Young children often have many thoughts and dreams about

what they want to be and do when they grow up. They'll usually change their minds many times. High schoolers, of course, need to get more focused when thinking about their post-high school experiences. Because the Internet has exposed them to so much and many of today's children are multitalented and often multipassionate, choosing college majors and career paths isn't as easy as it once was.[4]

Knowing how they're smart gives young people another answer to the "Who am I?" identity question so they can make decisions with more confidence. The question becomes what careers will best fit their interests, abilities, gifts, passions, *and* smarts? Also, because they're exposed to real-time, raw, unedited news everywhere all the time, they're aware of how much is wrong in the world. Therefore, asking *"What problems do you hope you can help solve?"* can be a very effective way of helping them identify interests and passions.[5]

Careers tend to be most fulfilling when there's a good match between the job skills and a person's smarts. Therefore, word-smart children may want to consider careers that involve speaking, listening, reading, and writing. Depending on their other smarts, debating and persuading can also be added to the mix. So, for example, careers with a good fit would include teacher, pastor, counselor, journalist, editor, lawyer, radio or television newsperson, librarian, and politician. Adults who are underemployed, unemployed, or dissatisfied with their work may also find it profitable to consider how they are smart when wanting to change their circumstances.[6]

RELATIONSHIPS

Gifts and Challenges

Although it's most common to first apply knowledge about children's smarts to their learning, the smarts are actually very relevant to friendships, as well. When children know how they are smart, they can more readily find others who they'll relate to well. This is partly because their smarts influence what they do in their spare time and what they want to talk about.

Word-smart children will often prioritize the sharing of knowledge in relationships. As a result, others will probably appreciate them for their knowledge and the meaningful conversations they can have with them. They're interested in both explaining what they know and learning from others.

Word-smart strengths may contribute to relationship challenges. These children may talk too much and negatively judge those who don't communicate clearly and deeply. Word-smart children can tend to look down on those they think don't know as much as they do. In addition, especially if they're also introverted, small talk may be very challenging for them because they'd rather be purposeful. This can confuse friends who always view them as talkers.

RELATING TO PARENTS:
WHEN IS TALKING TOO MUCH OF A GOOD THING?

Because many word-smart children admit to being distracted by the words in their own minds, you might want them to repeat aloud what you tell them, such as the steps to complete their project and the place you need them to put their toys. This may keep your relationship healthier because you'll be less frustrated and have increased success and decreased stress.

Word-smart children need you to listen closely to their stories and explanations about any number of things. You can comment on their observations and ask questions to indicate you are interested in the things they're passionate about. Providing them with appropriate, accurate books and other materials related to topics they're interested in shows them you're listening and that you care about them. Being available when they need to think aloud about something will increase their trust in you, motivation, and obedience.

But you also have a right to your space and quiet. So do siblings. Word-smart children must choose to respect others by not always having to talk. Teach your word-smart children that too much of a good thing isn't a good thing. Talking is good. Sharing is good. Conversations are good. Too much of it all the time is not good. Teaching and modeling this will likely result in permanent, positive behavior. Telling them over and over again to be quiet or worse, yelling it over and over, may paralyze this smart. That can result in permanent change of the worse kind—from God's intended design to a mere shadow of what could have been.

SPIRITUAL GROWTH

Learning and Listening

How can we help word-smart children who haven't yet trusted Christ for their salvation? And how can we help believing word-smart children continue to grow in their faith?

Realizing that other smarts, their spiritual gifts, interests, and passions will influence which spiritual disciplines they prefer, it's still safe to predict that reading and studying Scripture are probably important disciplines for word-smart children. Using more than one translation of the Bible and cross-referencing may increase their confidence in God and His Word. This is now easier than it used to be because of different websites and apps.

Because vocabulary tends to be one of their strengths, teaching them more about God by using His different names might be effective. They may also be interested to learn that the Bible was first written in Hebrew, Aramaic, and Greek. You could learn some of these words together.

Involve your children in family devotions rather than just doing it for them.

They will benefit from having their own Bible, Bible storybooks, Christian classics such as the Narnia

69

tales by C. S. Lewis, and devotional books. They may also be very interested in what you're learning, so take advantage of this.

Family devotions are important for all children, no matter their intelligence strengths. Children who are very word smart may enjoy them more and benefit from them more than others. It will be especially helpful if you involve them in the devotions rather than just doing devotions for them. Encourage them to read the Scripture and lesson aloud for everyone. They can also answer some questions and share relevant illustrations.

Because of their learning and listening strengths, word-smart children will also connect with God by attending church services, Sunday school, children's church, midweek church programs, retreats, youth seminars, and vacation Bible school.

CHARACTER:
BE SMART WITH YOUR WORD SMART

The Risk of Pride

Strengths can get us into trouble. For example, word-smart children can be prideful in their intellectual abilities and school grades. Feeling good about one's strengths is one thing, but feeling superior to others because of one's gifts is another. Word-smart children may want to show off their knowledge and/or vocabulary. They may be tempted to look down on others who don't appear to have strong literacy skills or who don't earn high grades. They may become unteachable, believing they know enough because they tend to be well read.

Do you know children who often struggle with word-smart-related sins? Word-smart children need to be careful of sins of the tongue such as gossiping, teasing, lying, and arguing. They need to be careful of always needing to have the last word or of talking when they should be listening. These negative behaviors can be easy for them. (Believe me, I know!)

Ideally you'll find ways to help them stop using their strengths in unhealthy ways without paralyzing, or shutting down, this intelligence. I'm grateful that didn't happen to me. If it had, I doubt Celebrate Kids, Inc., would have been founded or I'd be writing this book.

My parents knew I was a Chatty Kathy. They loved me as their daughter, accepted this part of me, and they liked me. I lost track a long time ago of how many children have told me they know their parents love them because they have to. They don't feel liked. The sadness and fear in their eyes sometimes haunts me.[7]

My parents could have seen my chattiness as a problem to eliminate, but they saw it as a strength to develop. What a beautiful perspective! Think about your child. Does he or she have a word-smart strength that sometimes irritates you or others? Does it interfere with friendships and academics? Have you been wanting to eliminate it? Trying? What if you chose to see the strength that's there and helped your son or daughter develop it for good? That's your power; your choice. Is what I'm observing a problem to eliminate or evidence of a strength to develop?

My parents looked for opportunities to help me use and develop my talents and interests. Even my brother and cousin got involved. When our grandfather was mayor, they published their own little newspaper called the *Cousins Gazette*.

I still have vivid memories of being a reporter on election nights. With my notepad and pencil, I circulated among the women on the first floor and the men in the basement of my grandparents' home, asking them the questions Dave and Terry assigned to me. As best I could, I wrote down their answers and composed an article, often with Dave's or Terry's help. I remember being thrilled at seeing my name in print when my articles were published.

When you're frustrated with the choices your children make, remember that sometimes emphasizing positive uses of abilities is more effective than talking about the problematic ones. Often!

So that's a look at the first of eight intelligences. Remember you can use the interactive online checklist whenever you want. It's available here: www.8GreatSmarts.com. You and others can rank each child based on the qualities that are associated with being word smart. It can be especially valuable to discover whether you and your child see him or her differently. If this happens, provide current evidence and ask your child to do the same. Evidence doesn't lie. If one of you needs to change opinions, listen and look for evidence this happens. For example, if your child needs to believe your evidence that he has improved his word smart, don't allow him to talk negatively about himself as he might have done in the past.

Let's Play!

Play *Scattergories*: If you can quickly come up with a list of, say, things at the park, in a drawer, and that you wear that start with the letter *t* that no one else thinks of, you can win this game.

Play *Apples to Apples*: One player draws a card. Each player selects a word card from their hand that they think is most relevant to the word on that card. If the judge picks your card, you win that round. Unlikely connections among words make for lots of laughter!

I AM LOGIC SMART:
I THINK WITH QUESTIONS

As an icebreaker, I asked adults to name an important place. Bonnie's answer, "The kitchen table," caused every head to snap in her direction. Some of the adults probably wondered if she heard my question correctly. Those with logic-smart strengths might have thought her answer was ridiculous or even wrong. They want everything to make sense, and her answer didn't—*to them.*

Bonnie had been to several countries on mission trips. In comparison, how could the kitchen table be an important place? I asked her about her choice. Bonnie explained that she credited her success and happiness to what she learned at the kitchen table talking with her parents and siblings.

Now her choice made sense. The logic-smart people were satisfied. Actually, I remember all of us being speechless and humbled.

Logic-smart people need things to make sense, but there's more to understand, so let's dig in. Remember that if you don't think logic smart is a strength for your children yet, your strategic involvement can strengthen it. Much of school success relies on logic-smart skills so it's important to cultivate as much of this intelligence as possible. It also has huge implications for a child's spiritual growth, as you'll see.

LOGIC SMART:
THE POWER OF REASONING

Logic-smart children think with questions. When they're excited, they ask more questions. They need things worth thinking about, things to make sense, and all their questions accepted. They get joy from solving intellectual puzzles and figuring things out. Reasoning is their power.

These children probably demonstrated common sense at a young age. Their strengths are rooted in thinking, and they might admit to thinking just for fun. This is definitely true of me. If friends ask "Do you want to have fun?" I can easily answer "Sure, what would you like to think about?" Because I know not everyone finds thinking fun, and small talk often satisfies others, I can choose to not verbalize all the questions that come to my mind while talking with friends at dinner or in the church lobby.

My great-aunt Ola liked thinking for fun and definitely noticed when things didn't make sense. She analyzed television commercials and after an ad for a brand of baking soda, I remember her laughing and laughing. The spokesperson was encouraging people to use baking soda to freshen the drain, so she directed, "Pour the box down the drain." Aunt Ola loved pointing out how that made no sense. "You can't pour the *box* down the drain!"

Children who are logic smart feel most secure when things make sense. Because this is their *need,* and they don't like to be confused, they may often ask "Why?" You may interpret these "Why?"

Much of school success relies on logic-smart skills so it's important to cultivate as much of this intelligence as possible.

questions as defiance, and they sometimes can be. But logic-smart children genuinely want to know why you don't want them to run in the backyard, why they're going to visit their cousins, or why you're serving spaghetti for dinner. Paralysis can certainly set in if you regularly answer their "Why?" questions with statements such as, *"Don't bother me now"* and *"I'll tell you if you need to know."*

Children with logic-smart strengths usually dive right in and explore new ideas. They can brainstorm questions easily, even helping parents think through vacation plans or other major decisions. Thinking isn't risky especially when they know the people they're with and they've proven to be trustworthy in the past.

These children might design systems and procedures for a

school club or keep statistics for their school's volleyball or basketball teams. Their ability to reason things through will help them be effective team leaders, perhaps for a church youth group. (Remember that intelligences don't work alone. Logic-smart children will be more effective leaders when they also have people-smart strengths.)

Thinking is so important to these children that if they're not kept challenged and engaged, they'll find something on their own to think about and analyze. For example, they may try taking apart color markers to determine why and how they work on only one type of paper. Do you understand why I often say bored logic-smart children can be dangerous?

Logic-smart children can also be dangerous when they're thinking! For instance, if you or your son's science teacher says, "Don't put those things in the bowl yet," how might your logic-smart son respond? Have you heard him ask, "Why not? What might happen?" If not, it's very possible he thought it and just didn't ask it out loud.

Before anyone realizes it, has your son put everything in the bowl to see what happens? Something will happen! Your response can either paralyze the logic-smart part of his mind or expand and develop it further. It's okay to respond, because he was disobedient, but can you picture and even hear in your mind a response that could shut down his logic-smart thinking and one that would honor and strengthen it?

LEARNING MATTERS:
QUESTIONS, QUESTIONS

I classify logic smart as another "school smart." Written questions and discussion questions are a part of virtually every class. Assignments using questions are common. Also, tests using all types of questions have become an even more prevalent and significant way children are judged than in the past. There's more, though. Science and math are usually enjoyed by logic-smart children and these are key subjects for many years of school.

On one hand, school is designed for them. But all the questions can backfire. Logic-smart children need something worth thinking about. If they're bored, material is reviewed too often so it's too easy, or students judge the topics or assignments as irrelevant, they can mentally check out. They're physically present, but mentally absent. The use of questions doesn't guarantee success.

Homeschooling may work well for logic-smart children. They can explore topics they're interested in at a pace that works. Their questions (which they *always* have!) can be answered more regularly. Not only can time be used more flexibly, they have more access to parents at home and teachers in cooperatives than they would teachers in classrooms. They can also demonstrate their understanding in a variety of ways so they'll be successful. If you don't homeschool, you'll want to be fully present so your children can ask you questions after school.

As is demonstrated by the "Don't put those things in the bowl yet" illustration, many logic-smart children like discovering things on their own. Science usually inspires them. They like exploring and experimenting. Their strengths lie in their accurate, research-driven, and cause-effect thinking. They're good at analyzing, predicting, and inventing.

Our reactions to their questions can either increase their logic or shut it down.

Math is usually a strength of these children because they appreciate its logic. For instance, 2+2 = 4, 22+22 = 44, and 222+222 = 444. Always. Math strengths might be obvious early, when numbers, adding, telling time, and understanding money didn't frustrate your son. As he gets older, you might see that estimating and statistics (e.g., professional baseball stats) are strengths. This might be why he is drawn to certain apps and uses of technology.

Success with some types of math depends on other intelligences. For example, word-smart skills are necessary for story problems and picture-smart strengths help children learn shapes and geometry. Plus, because of other learning styles or attention issues, memorizing math facts might not be easy. That doesn't mean these children aren't logic smart. They may just need to grow into it. Next week or next semester, math might be easier because of the type of math assigned and the smarts they can use. Remember it's not an all or nothing model. Degrees of logic smartness exist in all of us.

Strengthening Logic Smart: Asking "What If?"

The asking of questions is an essential life skill and it's one of the most important reasons to awaken this intelligence early. If children tend to *not* ask questions, introducing them to fun trivia and fascinating facts can encourage them to do so. Our reactions to their questions can either increase their logic or shut it down. If you don't want to discourage logic-smart investigations, don't respond like this: *"You don't need to know that." "Look it up yourself." "That's not important."* Many adults have told me they remember being told these things often and credit these responses for paralyzing their logic smart. Instead, respond like this: *"I never would have thought of that question! You like figuring things out and I'm glad." "I don't know the answer either. After dinner, remind me and we'll research the answer. I want to know, too."*

Having problems to solve will further awaken and strengthen this smart. Children will benefit from "What-if?" thinking. Statements that begin with "I wonder . . ." can also stimulate their curiosity and engage their logic-smart minds. Because reasoning is their power, ask them why and how they came up with their statements, answers, and solutions. Interact with them to grow their reasoning strengths.

Teaching what different thinking verbs mean and using the verbs carefully can be especially helpful. This is also productive and motivational for children who already have logic-smart strengths.

You don't have to think about separating children in order to use this and other ideas. Your reasons to use the ideas may be different (e.g., awaken *and* strengthen) and one child may be quicker to respond than another, but everyone can benefit.

Rather than telling children to "just think" about their reading assignment or while watching a video, it's wise to tell them how to *specifically* think and to make sure they know how to think in those ways. If your children don't know what the thinking verbs on tests and assignments mean, they won't do well even if they know the material. That's sad. For instance, you can ask them to listen or read so they can distinguish, evaluate, and predict. We can teach the differences between compare and contrast and evaluate and judge. And what exactly should children do when told to speculate, defend, and interpret?[1]

Learning Struggles: When Rules Don't Work

Most young children enjoy fiction and make-believe stories. As they grow up, if they are picture smart, they'll continue to enjoy all kinds of fiction and uses of their imagination. However, if your daughter is more logic smart than picture smart, she may struggle if you teach her to read using mostly fiction. Using nonfiction sometimes is wise. Because children with logic-smart strengths like it when things make sense, their interests typically lie more with nonfiction than fiction and report writing more than story writing.

Have you chosen one story to read to two children and one likes it and the other thinks it's dumb? Maybe your son found the talking animals enjoyable and your daughter kept thinking, "Animals don't talk!!" In contrast, because logic-smart children are natural problem solvers, mysteries might be their favorite fiction. They also might prefer these types of television shows.

Because logic-smart children can struggle when things don't make sense and when "rules" don't work, spelling and phonics can challenge them. Unless logic-smart children are also picture smart and they can remember what the words look like, they may struggle. This can be true even if they are word smart.

For example, even though many children are still taught that when two vowels are together, the first vowel makes the long sound, the letters "ea" can make numerous sounds: st*ea*k, m*ea*l, d*ea*d, *ea*rly, r*ea*ct. Even with the same exact letters in a word, the sound "ea" changes: "r*ea*d" and "r*ea*d." And "red" is also pronounced like "read." No wonder some children struggle to learn how to read! And then there are words like "there," "their," and "they're." These, too, can discourage logic-smart children.

Spelling doesn't come naturally to me. Word smart and logic smart are both strengths of mine. I want the rules to work and get frustrated when they don't. Because picture smart is one of my weakest smarts, I don't think with my eyes. I can't remember what the word looked like the last time I saw it. Was there a "c" after the "s"? Did the word have a double "f" or a double "s" or were both doubled?

I definitely rely on the spell-check feature in my computer, my misspeller's dictionary, thesaurus and dictionary websites, staff members who proof some of my work before I send it out, and editors. Why do I use a thesaurus if my problem is spelling? Because that's how I sometimes find words I want to use that I'm not sure how to spell. I look up "famous" to find "acclaimed" (one "c" or two?) and "renowned." (Is it spelled with a "u" or a "w"?) It's much more efficient than trying to find words I can't spell in a dictionary.

Even though spelling is not a natural strength for me, I'm a writer. We must be obedient. Because God has called me to write, I write. No excuses! I work to remember words I use often and humble myself by relying on others. Children can do this, too. "I must not let my weaknesses win. I must lead with my strengths!"

I ask children in my programs if I'm stupid because something challenges me. They quickly shout, "Nooooo!" Then I ask them if they're stupid if something is hard for them. They have to shout, "Nooooo!" It's a powerful moment.

Support your child. Make sure he or she understands that we will all have topics, assignments, and academic subjects that challenge us. Having eight smarts doesn't mean everything is easy, but it does mean children have more internally to rely on than they thought they do. And, so do you!

One more thing. Did you notice how I worded my issue with spelling? I wrote, "Spelling doesn't come naturally to me." As I wrote about in chapter 1, identity controls behavior. When something is a weakness, it's important that you give thought to how to express it. What we believe, what children hear us say, and what we allow them to say all matter. For example, imagine how children react to word-smart tasks if we allow them to define themselves in these ways: *"Spelling is hard"* or *"I'm not good at spelling"* or *"I can't spell."*

Teaching the Logic-Smart Child: Let's Explore!

To study and learn best with their logic-smartness, children should ask and answer questions. Therefore, as often as you can, take advantage of children's expressed curiosity, even when their questions appear to be off-task. Also, help them think through and research answers to their own questions. This can further grow their curiosity, knowledge, and logic-smart thinking skills.

To engage the logic-smart part of the mind, use brainteasers, experiments across the curriculum, time lines, research, data collections, debate, and numbers in more than math classes. Providing objects and ideas to explore and think about can further awaken and expand the logic-smart part of children's minds. Open-ended exploration, where many conclusions can result, will be an especially good starting place. Field trips, so they can observe and interact with knowledge firsthand, also enhance this intelligence.[2]

If logic-smart children's reading skills aren't strong, they can become frustrated because they're genuinely interested in truth. Plus they typically want to do well in school. Sometimes reading books about the same topic, but written at an easier level, will help them handle their reading assignments more successfully. These easier materials will make their grade-level texts manageable by introducing needed vocabulary words and background knowledge. For example, college students can read high school-level texts, and middle school and high school students can find the same topics covered in textbooks for younger students or in library books. You can also read relevant material to them. Websites and YouTube videos can help, too.

WHEN THEY GROW UP:
CAREERS AND EDUCATION

Logic-smart children may be most fulfilled in careers that involve using their logic-smart mind. Because of their ability to formulate and ask questions and then critique answers, counseling, teaching, researching, and careers involving public safety such as police work and forensic science may appeal to them. If they are also body smart, then careers like auto mechanic, plumber, and utility worker make sense. STEM-related (science, technology, engineering, mathematics) careers come to mind. Other intelligence strengths, passions, and spiritual gifts can influence which of these will be the best fit: clinical chemist, pharmacist, electrician, accountant, insurance/risk management, appraiser, banker, and meteorologist.

RELATIONSHIPS:
HELPING OTHERS SOLVE PROBLEMS

Since solving problems is a definite strength of logic-smart children, and it's often part of their identity and reputation, this may be the basis for their belonging. Because they provide accurate and helpful information and commonsense advice, those with significant needs or with immature problem-solving skills may choose them as friends. They're usually excellent at brainstorming and can help others think of new questions that enhance their understandings and academic success.

Logic-smart questioning and problem-solving strengths can easily become a stumbling block when taken to the extreme. For example, logic-smart children may only want to relate to those who have problems because they feel important and better about themselves when they help them. This, of course, isn't healthy.

These children may also want to be right all the time. They may think they can reason better than others so their ideas must be right—or *more* right than yours or their friends' ideas. They may push their ideas and keep asking questions to intimidate others. They may be very good at arguing. A mom recently shared this with me: *I have a very word-smart child who is also strong willed and logic smart. After [learning about how she is smart], I was able not to be dragged into her fights. I would remind her that she needed to use her words for good. And that I would be happy to talk with her but I wasn't going to argue. She was thirteen or fourteen at the time, and she was shocked the next time she was ready to argue and I walked away. She is now eighteen, we seldom argue, and I am often told of the kind words she shows to others.*

Humor can be challenging for logic-smart children. Some of them may judge humor and some forms of fun as unnecessary or frivolous. They often think things are stupid that other children find funny. This can be stressful because they don't laugh when others do, and they can feel like they don't fit in.

Small talk can bore or frustrate them, since they want to talk about things worth thinking about. There are times when I'm at dinner with friends and I think of things to say or questions to ask and I don't. The conversation would turn too serious for some. I choose to have self-control and respect for others and stay engaged in the conversation. This honors my friends and is right. There are times when I do speak up and my friends enjoy thinking with me. I just have to sense when it's right. It helps that I'm people smart and can read body language and facial expressions. You'll want to prioritize awakening and strengthening this smart in your child.

You'll also want to make sure your child does have logic-smart friends. These are the ones your son can discuss current events with. You can invite some to go to the museum with your family. Your daughter will know to choose from among these when looking for friends to help her plan a Valentine's banquet at the nursing home where her grandparents live.

These children may want to be right all the time.

Although it may be more common with logic-smart adults than children, these children also need to be careful of analyzing people rather than loving them. Many years ago, a friend of mine sent me a letter to explain that our friendship was at risk. I was surprised, but as I read her letter, she made total sense. We became friends during a time in her life when she benefited from my problem-solving skills. She talked about what was going on, and I asked questions and provided solutions. It became a natural rhythm for our conversations. However, in her letter, she explained that she felt like a problem I was trying to solve or a project I was trying to finish. She asked me to listen and love her instead. (I know from many conversations I've had that this can be an issue with husbands and wives.)

I remain grateful to this day that my friend trusted me with her pain, believed I could change, and didn't just end our friendship. I would have missed her. After many weeks of honest conversations and some important decisions, a new rhythm was established and we are closer today than we were then. For a long time, I prayed before calling her, asking God to enhance my listening skills and compassion while temporarily quieting my questioning and solution-oriented focus. She still values my problem-solving abilities, but doesn't need them often. When she does share a dilemma with me, I wait for her to ask for assistance before I offer any ideas.

Relating to Parents: Loving with Heart and Mind

Children tell me their parents often interact with them as I did with my friend. Some admit they're glad their parents have problem-solving and thinking strengths, but there are times when they'd just like to be heard and not analyzed. Some admit they stop sharing with their parents to avoid the inevitable interrogation and problem-solving session. Is this relevant in your family dynamic? Make sure your children know you love and appreciate them and don't view them as problems or projects even though they may have problems. Love them with your heart *and* your mind.[3]

If your son is word smart and people smart, he will need to talk in order to problem solve. If he doesn't think he can with you, you're not just paralyzing his logic smart but possibly these other two smarts, as well. Make sure to remember the encouraging truth from chapter 2. Intelligences can be reawakened. If you believe I'm describing a recent family dynamic, talk about it. You could even read these paragraphs to your son to facilitate the discussion. Humbly include that you didn't intend to use your strengths to discourage or defeat him.

Over-answering children's questions isn't the only way to negatively affect your relationship with your logic-smart child. Dismissing their questions and not allowing them to explore safe things they want to think about can also shut down this intelligence. In contrast, researching and exploring with them what they're curious about and providing relevant and accurate information will positively affect these children. A sure way to increase their security in you is to be one of those who helps them learn to handle confusion, seeming

Logic is not enough for a complete connection with God.

contradictions, and other things that violate their need for logic. If you get frustrated during difficult times and don't enjoy confusion, admit it. Teach your child how you cope when things don't appear to make sense. Demonstrate that you can be calm in the midst of storms. Teach how you've learned to get along with people who aren't consistent or as logical as you'd prefer.

SPIRITUAL GROWTH: SEARCHING FOR TRUTH

Logic-smart children will most likely appreciate God for His truth and wisdom. In fact, they must be careful of the tendency to be satisfied with merely knowing *about* God. They must move on to knowing God, believing in God, and loving God. They may struggle with principles like grace, mercy, and unconditional love.

91

Studying these and having them explained and modeled can help children understand and believe in these heart principles. Logic is not enough for a complete connection with God; they also need the heart's feelings and responses.

Logic-smart children may be fascinated and comforted by the logic and consistency between the Old and New Testaments (e.g., prophecies in the Old that have been proven true in the New, the God of Daniel is the same as the God of Revelation). The consistency of the four Gospels and the recurring themes in Paul's writings are also relevant to these children. Because they love to learn, they may want to read more than the Bible. They'll probably prefer nonfiction books to "cute devotionals." They might dig deeply into one subject, reading several books on prayer, for example, and/or they may choose to read and study everything by one author they like.

A study of Job will show them there's nothing wrong with searching for truth and in asking tough questions. They'll also see that faith is possible even when we don't understand everything. This is, perhaps, the greatest challenge for logic-smart children. Christianity doesn't always make a lot of sense! Logic-smart children should be told they don't need to know everything about God in order to believe Him or to believe in Him.

Much of the harm done in the world is done by logic-smart people who are really stupid.

Understanding this was very important in my own faith journey.

For logic-smart children to trust Christ for their salvation, their parents, pastors, Sunday school teachers, and small-group leaders must be open to hearing any and all questions the children have about God, spiritual issues, and themselves. Children must have their questions honored. Parents can research answers with them by using Bible study tools and talking with pastors and Sunday school teachers.

CHARACTER:
BE SMART WITH YOUR LOGIC SMART

Analyzing—and Worrying

Intellectual pride (believing they have all the answers) and spiritual pride (believing they have figured out God) can be character flaws. Judging others, arguing to make their points and to defend themselves, and being angry when they're confused are other sin temptations.

Logic-smart children may also tend to worry because thinking and analyzing come easily to them, and they like it when things make sense. I can relate to this. I've joked with friends and coworkers, telling them, "I'm analyzing." But it's not funny. Sin is sin. I might call it analyzing, but sometimes I'm worrying.

If you think your child may have this tendency, I encourage you to talk about it. Many children have told me after my programs that they worry or are anxious and don't like it. They have felt guilty and weak and like they don't have enough faith. They can learn, from you, that they're okay. And, you can help them handle uncertainties better in the future as you model how you do it and as you make yourself available for any and all questions.

Logic-smart children's problem-solving abilities can easily ensnare them if they're not careful. In my programs about this topic for children, I often include that much of the harm done in the world is done by logic-smart people who are really stupid. They laugh. Then it sinks in. Logic-smart children must be very careful. It's easier than we think to cross over the line from good to harm. Not only can logic-smart children solve problems, they can create them—often without being caught.

Logic-smart children can also get into trouble by challenging and testing adults. Children laugh with me when I ask them what they might think if a parent ordered, "Don't step over that line!" I demonstrate by putting one foot over an imaginary line and saying: "I'm not all the way over the line. I'm straddling it. I know. I looked the word up in a dictionary. It won't be right if my dad gets mad. And if I step *on* the line, I'm also not over the line. If I do that and get yelled at, I'll just tell my dad he's wrong." The amount of laughter indicates that many children think like that! I then make the important point that they have a responsibility to do what's right. Intelligence strengths are no excuse for sin. Obedience is right!

Let's Play!

Play *Blokus*: Players take turns placing pieces of their chosen color on the board. It's tricky because each new piece must touch at least one other piece of the same color, but only at the corners. You win if you place more pieces than anyone else.

Play *Clue*: Crack the murder that took place in the mansion by asking the right questions to win this classic game. Junior version available.

I AM PICTURE SMART: I THINK WITH PICTURES

Kristin attended one of my multiple intelligence seminars for parents and teachers years after being one of my college students. It was great to see her again. She was now thirty years old and teaching dance to children. After the seminar, I received a long, handwritten letter from her.

Here's part of what Kristin wrote:

By the time I was a sophomore in high school, I was pretty broken. The classes I excelled at, such as creative writing and history, seemed to be few and far between. The required classes like algebra and chemistry slew me. I can't tell you how many tears I shed. I was, in my own opinion, and seemingly in the opinions of my teachers, not very smart. C grades were common in math and science. As for the occasional As I did receive, those came out of classes like choir and other subjects that came easily to me. I never imagined that kind of information was easy for me to process because I was smart. I thought the material was easy.

As a junior in the second-rate history course, I watched one day as my history teacher stood in front of our class and assisted us in deciding which courses to take the following year. He was careful to mention that Western civilization was a very difficult course, and he didn't think that any of us would enjoy it. To prove his point, he cited examples that were supposed to discourage us. "I mean—you have to learn all this stuff like who painted the Mona Lisa and . . ." Before I knew what I was doing, I said, "da Vinci." Mr. Green looked at me. My classmates looked at me. I, relatively shy, swallowed and let Mr. Green bring it back on track with "Well, more than that. You have to know stuff like who designed Monticello." I matter-of-factly said, "Thomas Jefferson." Mr. Green looked at me. My classmates looked at me. He continued, "You have to know stuff like who painted the ceiling of the Sistine Chapel." Without missing a beat, I responded, "Michelangelo." None of the answers came out of impertinence. They came out of surprise. Weren't these answers common knowledge?

After all was said and done, I had answered all of the questions well-intending Mr. Green was trying to use to dissuade us. The catch of this little story? After getting those sample questions right, I decided not to take the class. Why? Well, everyone said it was really hard and only the smart kids took it. So I didn't. No one came to me and said, "Boy, you're picture smart and have the ability to analyze details. This is the class for you!" For the record, I later took a similar class in college and aced it!

Can you relate to anything Kristin shared? Do your children know the answers to Mr. Green's questions, and do they understand they're smart if they do? Do you see how helpful being picture smart can be even though these abilities are downplayed in many schools? Can you feel how discouraging it can be when these strengths are devalued?

PICTURE SMART: A PORTRAIT

Picture-smart children think with pictures. When they're excited, they add to their pictures. They need freedom to doodle/draw and their creativity respected. They get joy from being lost in the process of creating. Visualizing and observing are their powers.

Children with picture-smart strengths pay attention to and think with visuals *in books*, such as pictures, diagrams, maps, charts, and illustrations. That's how Kristin knew the answers to Mr. Green's questions. They also notice and think with things they see in their environment. When I write that these children think "in pictures," that includes anything visual. Is this an interest for your child? A strength?

Picture-smart children also visualize pictures, diagrams, and colors *in their minds*. For example, if you easily create visuals for the words that follow, it's because you're picture smart: candle, stagecoach, and volcano. Because everyone is picture smart to some extent, everyone can create some kind of visuals for these words. Very picture-smart children will *want* to create them and they'll do it easily, using accurate details and rich colors. Others of us might need to make a concerted effort to merely sketch outlines in our minds, and it will take time for us to do so.

Picture-smart children usually have more artistic abilities than visual learners and they think with their visuals.

Especially if you homeschool your children, you may be familiar with the concept that children can be visual learners. Picture-smart children are gifted differently from them just as auditory learners are not the same as word-smart learners. Picture-smart children usually have more artistic abilities than visual learners and they *think with* their visuals. Visual learners *remember* what they see. It's possible to have strengths in one, both, or neither of these learning styles. Both may visualize.

In my "Eight Great Smarts" school programs, I ask children who can see a volcano when I just say the word, and about 75 percent of the children raise their hands. I then ask them to describe the color of the lava as it erupts. I'm often impressed with how quickly and confidently many of them can do this. *"It's mostly red-orange with some ruby red sections." "Mine is more orange-red and it's almost fluorescent where it's hottest." "Some sections of my lava are so dark, they look black."*

When picture-smart children get excited, they tell me they add to the pictures in their minds—another color and shape in the design or another animal getting sucked into lava. They also tell me *"the movie in my mind plays faster."* They'll also doodle or create faster or with more colors, details, and designs on actual paper when they're excited.

Those who are very picture smart don't intend for words and sights to trigger visuals that pop into their minds. It just happens automatically. Just as word-smart children automatically talk when excited and logic-smart children ask questions without being prompted, children with picture-smart strengths visualize automatically. Often, the visuals help their comprehension, retention, and enjoyment, but this ability can backfire. When the images are irrelevant to the lessons, they don't help. Besides that, they can cause children to daydream.

The pictures they see in their minds also contribute to their keen sense of humor. They often admit to seeing things that probably weren't intended. This is sometimes awkward as they laugh in the middle of serious discussions. When you think this is the cause of their laughter, it can be fun to ask them what they just saw. I've had children respond with, *"How did you know?"* and *"Did you see it, too?"* Both can stimulate a beneficial discussion about how they are smart and how to use self-control at times like this.

Picture-smart children have possibly referred to themselves as creative, artistic, interested in beauty, and talented. You have the privilege now of letting them know they are these things because they are smart. This intelligence may not be considered a "school smart" by most people because these abilities are not as highly valued in the system. But it adds joy to life and is essential for the children God chose it for. We want these children to stop thinking they're not smart but others are. Tell them they're smart! This is your power!

When picture-smart children value their abilities, they might develop their skills so they can serve as photographers for their school's website, designers for their school yearbook, and wardrobe and stage assistants for their school's spring musical. They might create flyers used to advertise school events. They can arrange furniture, hang appropriate posters, and adjust the lighting in the church youth room to make the atmosphere inviting.

The hierarchy of intelligence is evident with this smart as it is with the others. All picture-smart children can see and design in their minds. They can also sketch, draw, or paint. Some do it better than others; that's part of the hierarchy. Others are into flowcharts and diagrams and are more likely to draw intricate designs and build with blocks. There are some who struggle to do any of this.

Some children were doing much of this and stopped because of reactions from parents, siblings, and others. Parents might have discovered blocks everywhere and consistently demanded, *"Pick those up!"* Or they may see doodles and drawings and ask, *"Aren't you going to do anything important today?"* Hello paralysis!

Paralysis of the picture smart can also occur due to technology. Children might game all the time or spend all their time scrolling social media sites. They'll have no time to draw, create, or imagine anymore. It's absolutely essential that you set boundaries for your children and make sure they don't use only digital devices when they have spare time.[1]

Watch carefully, though. It's possible that your early doodler has now become a master at certain games requiring picture-smart skills. They might actually be increasing his interest and improving his ability. It's also possible your son watches movies in part to critique the design, colors, and sets and because he has a vivid picture-smart ability to imagine. In these ways, technology is good. Still, it's always best to keep a healthy balance between "screens" and other activities.

LEARNING MATTERS:
THE POWER TO OBSERVE

Children with picture-smart strengths probably enjoy creative writing, fiction, and history. The action comes alive in their mind's eye. Action also comes alive when they read the Bible to themselves or someone reads it to them. These are the children who have seen the coat of many colors, Jonah in the fish, and Jesus walking on water. Ask your child about this. You might be very encouraged by his or her vivid descriptions. Your son might also laugh when he sees Jesus turning into a piece of bread as you're teaching that Jesus is "the bread of life" (John 6:35). I'll never forget one child who declared, *"And, Dr. Kathy, He is not boring white bread! He is multi-grain bread like my mom makes me eat!"* Just as with your responses to the logic-smart experimenter you're raising, responses to comments like these from picture-smart children can either paralyze the intelligence or encourage children to use it more. As I often teach, the words we speak and the words we don't speak change lives. We must be alert and careful!

It's absolutely essential that you set boundaries for your children and make sure they don't use only digital devices when they have spare time.

The picture-smart power to observe is valuable in many classes. In math, observation skills might mean that a plus sign is not misread as a minus sign. Picture-smart children can better understand geometry problems because they can picture the lines intersecting as the teacher describes them. In science, a chemical's structure can still be seen in children's minds after closing their textbooks. In art, they will notice size and not just color. In music, they won't miss the flat sign in front of the note.

Picture-smart strengths can make letter and number identification easier for young children. That's one reason it definitely pays to activate this part of the brain early in life. For children who struggle to discern between "b and d," "was and saw," and/or "6 and 9," you want to strengthen their picture-smart skills rather than simply drilling them on these letters, words, and numbers.

Picture-smart strengths also help children succeed in athletics. I think of my niece Katie. She was an excellent college scholarship soccer player and now she's a high school coach of different sports. When playing soccer, she could more accurately picture the trajectory of the ball after it's kicked than the athlete who lacks picture-smart abilities. As a coach, she is able to picture the play she wants her athletes to execute so she teaches it well.

Remember that we always rely on more than one intelligence at a time. For instance, if children with picture-smart strengths are also very body smart, they'll probably have excellent eye-hand coordination. Therefore, they'll have legible handwriting and create sculptures more readily than others could. They may also enjoy taking things apart and putting them back together. Being logic smart may also help with this.

There's more. A picture-smart, logic-smart combination can make geometry easier. This can show up early, when only some young children easily learn that squares and rectangles are different.

Trigonometry, calculus, and advanced algebra are also math disciplines in which children will need to use picture-smart skills. An important implication follows. Children who want to improve their understanding and grades in these courses may be well advised to develop their picture-smartness in addition to working on math principles.

Strengthening Picture Smart: "Close Your Eyes and See"

Starting when your child is very young, you can color together, have fun finger painting even if they're older, and experiment by making several kinds of Jell-O together. What color will it be and how will it taste? Build with Play Doh, popsicle sticks, and Legos. All of this and more will further awaken this smart.

Reading picture books together and stopping to admire the artistry can be effective. Point out how the choices of color, facial expressions, and little things in the background enrich the story and your enjoyment. Occasionally go to art museums and craft shows together. You won't want to overdo this or expect your child to necessarily enjoy these experiences as much as you do, but these times can further awaken this smart. Just have realistic expectations so you're not disappointed. If your child senses any frustration on your part, these activities could backfire and paralysis could actually set in.

As children are listening and studying, you can tell them to

"Close your eyes and see." They can see the word they're trying to learn, data they're trying to memorize, and the order of events for their history test. You can also say, *"Picture this"* at the beginning of your instructions. When doing homework and taking tests, children can learn to ask themselves, *"Does it look right?"* Teachers and parents can also ask this question to stimulate picture-smart thinking. Even those of us without much of this smart benefit from drawing upon it. But we almost always have to be reminded to do it because it's not natural.

Choosing to visualize has enhanced my understanding of Scripture and improved my memory work. The word "choosing" is a key. Naturally gifted picture-smart learners don't have to choose to visualize. The visuals will automatically appear in their minds, often whether they want them to or not. However, some of us need to make a conscious choice to think with our eyes. Picture smart will never be in my top four or even six, but I have more of it now than I did even six months ago.

Learning Struggles: Helping Them Focus

Because so much time in school is spent thinking and talking about words and numbers, picture-smart children who don't have strengths with these may struggle. Not all words and numbers conjure up visual images, so they can become frustrated and bored. Listening for long stretches is challenging, and learning fatigue can set in.

This may be among the reasons Kristin didn't think she was smart.

When children intentionally use more than one intelligence, their learning will almost always be more accurate and they will retain information longer. They'll also be able to use the information more strategically. Imagine teaching math facts with word smart, logic smart, and picture smart at the same time. For example, a curriculum called "Times Tables the Fun Way" successfully uses stories and pictures to teach math facts. For the fact 6x6 = 36, they use a clever picture with this story: Two sixes walked across the hot desert to visit their cousin. When they arrived, they were very thirsty sixes. What's 6x6? Thirsty-six![2]

Sometimes strengths can actually cause learning problems. For example, children who are picture smart may decide that "monkey" is spelled m-o-n-k-e-y because there's a "tail" at the end of the word, just like a monkey has a tail. Then what might happen? They might read "money," "Mikey," and "many" as "monkey," because these words also have "tails." They might learn "elephant" on their vocabulary list only because it's the longest word. They won't know it when it's placed among other long words.

Picture-smart children can use their visual strengths to examine objects and pay close attention during demonstrations. They can learn a lot from these and they'll probably retain the information. However, children also tell me that some objects and demonstrations are so engaging and distracting that they interfere with their ability to pay attention to their teachers' instructions at the same time. Add some silence when they can just observe and study with their eyes.

Teaching the Picture-Smart Child: Watching and Creating

To activate and strengthen the picture-smart part of the brain when learning and studying, encourage activities that involve watching, creating, and visualizing. Focus on pictures, diagrams, maps. Children can also build things they see using pipe cleaners, clay, and the like. Children can be encouraged to use a camera to capture and critique different objects, people, and events. Help children notice descriptive words and details in lectures, videos, and written materials because they can paint the pictures in their minds.[3]

It's appropriate to use visuals throughout the curriculum. For example, as an in-class activity or homework assignment, children can draw the definition of vocabulary or spelling words. If they're studying different structures and their vocabulary words are *apartment building, condominium, duplex, warehouse,* and *factory,* one night they could sketch each structure. On another, their assignment could be to write definitions of each word. On another, they could be challenged to use all the words in one meaningful story. Children with picture-smart strengths will enjoy the drawing and creative writing tasks and benefit from them. Other children will profit because it uses a part of the mind that may not naturally engage while learning vocabulary. This will improve their understanding and memory. It's not necessary to evaluate the quality of the drawing, just the accuracy. In other words, does the apartment building look more like a warehouse? Is the duplex distinguishable from a house? Be careful here. A quick way to paralyze the picture smart is to ask, while looking at a picture, "What is that?" Rather, when we're unsure, we can learn to say "Tell me about your picture."

Another effective approach is to use thinking verbs that tend to activate and strengthen picture-smart reasoning and reflecting, such as *create, demonstrate, describe, illustrate,* and *show*.[4] When reading their texts and reviewing their notes, children can make up statements or questions their teachers might use on tests. For example, "*Illustrate* the process used to make paper." "*Describe* the story's setting, including details that, if changed, would have changed the story's outcome." "How could you *demonstrate* the same level of faith Daniel had?" If you're familiar enough with what your children are studying, you can make up questions and statements like these, too.

WHEN THEY GROW UP:
CAREERS AND EDUCATION

What might picture-smart children best succeed at after graduating from high school? What might be fulfilling? Other intelligence strengths will strongly influence this. For instance, if they're picture smart and body smart, they may want to investigate careers that involve their eyes and large- and/or small-motor skills (e.g., cartographer, construction worker, book illustrator, clothing designer, and photographer). A nature-smart strength might combine with picture-smart skills to make urban planning, horticulture, landscape architecture, and navigating appealing.

Not all "picture strengths" are the same. Your child might have abilities in the areas of color, art, design, or diagrams. Consider how these differences will influence the following career possibilities: art teacher, geometry teacher, graphic designer, sculptor, interior designer, movie or video game producer, pilot, surveyor, fashion designer, or architect.

RELATIONSHIPS:
UNDERSTANDING DIFFERENCES

Just like adults, children benefit from having a variety of friends. Sometimes we connect well with those who are very different from us. That's most likely when we know ourselves well, are confident, and have values and goals in common. Wanting to mature helps, too.

Some of my best friends are very picture smart. When a special exhibit was at one of our local art museums, I agreed to go with them. They enjoyed helping me appreciate the paintings and I enjoyed the experience. I wouldn't have enjoyed going alone, but

111

I'm glad I trusted my friends. I honored them and they helped me.

Nancy, one of my best friends and a member of my staff, is very picture smart. Consequently, she thinks well when doodling and sketching. When I know we'll be brainstorming over dinner, I bring pens of different colors and usually more than one kind of paper. It's a simple way I can encourage her. I'm satisfied with black ink and I rarely doodle, but Nancy isn't me. Expecting her to behave like me would be dishonoring and disrespectful. She doesn't always use the different pens, but she's glad they're available.

Your relationship will be strongest when you take your child's skills and interests seriously.

Help your child understand that different ways of approaching tasks is different, not wrong. Help him or her not judge others and assume that differences mean they can't get along or work together. Nancy and I have great times together and work productively. She has ideas I don't and I have unique ideas, too. We need each other. We respect each other.

Can you relate to my experiences? Share with your child so he or she knows it's more than possible to enjoy and benefit from peers who have different smart strengths.

Your picture-smart child will probably identify others like him or her by their creativity and humor. If they're in classes together, they might have noticed they like the same type of assignments. They might discover they like movies and apps with a high visual appeal. They might find out they enjoy crafts and photography and posting pictures on social media sites.

Relating to Parents: The Gift of Affirmation

Remember Kristin—she didn't know it was because she is smart that she knew answers to her teacher's questions. One of the best things you can do for your daughter is to let her know she is picture smart if she's creative, artistic, and good at thinking and observing with her eyes. Tell your son he's good at design and building what he sees in his mind because he is picture smart. When you affirm and build up your son and daughter, they will trust you, want to show you their work, and be more open to your helpful suggestions. "Smart" is a power word. Use it.

Your relationship will be strongest when you take your child's skills and interests seriously. This could involve helping him or her find ways to serve with this smart and ways to further develop picture-smart skills that are clear strengths. This might include trips to art festivals, birthday presents of art lessons or art supplies, connecting your son with architects and engineers as mentors, making weekly visits to a building site to notice progress and design elements, and volunteering as a family to help your church paint and decorate a house for an elderly couple.

You can use rich and descriptive language when disciplining and motivating your daughter. This will help her form pictures in her mind of what you do and do not want her to do. Also, letting her draw solutions for behavior problems may be helpful, as might letting her doodle while you talk with her.

Through the years I've been intrigued by how many children with picture-smart gifts tell me they don't want to look at their parents during difficult discussions. They explain that they may never be able to forget the disappointment in their dad's eyes or the anger in their mom's face, so they'd rather not see it. I encourage you to think about this and ask your child if this might be why he or she sometimes prefers not to make eye contact with you.

SPIRITUAL GROWTH

Connecting with the Creator

I believe God frequently uses our intelligence strengths when communicating with us. Therefore, you may hear picture-smart children declare, *"I saw what I'm supposed to do." "God showed me the next step." "I know what to do. I can see myself trying out for first chair!"* You need to take these statements seriously and not reject them simply because God may not communicate with you in the same way. Helping children believe in and take these visual promptings seriously is extremely important to their growing trust in God.

Since picture-smart children value their creativity, they may connect well to God as their Creator and resonate with Scriptures such as Genesis 1:27; Psalm 51:10; Ephesians 2:10; and

Colossians 1:16. They can be very inspired when they understand they are made in His image, and He is the source of their creativity.

These children think about God with pictures and their eyes, just as they think about everything else. Therefore, stained-glass windows, art, jewelry, picture books, and movies might draw them to God. Imagine you and your child examining different paintings of the Last Supper or different cross necklaces. Whether done in art museums, stores, or with pictures in books or catalogs, the discussions would be rich!

Descriptive Scriptures might be most engaging for these children. They may find especially appealing and instructive many of the Psalms, accounts of Old Testament heroes and battles, and Jesus' parables, object lessons, and miracles. Check out the *Picture-Smart Bible*.[5] It might be perfect for them!

Reading a Bible translation like *The Message* that reads more naturally than other translations may motivate and help picture-smart children become more interested in and mature in their faith. So might the *Amplified Bible*, because it includes more than one acceptable translation of the original Greek and Hebrew words. These additional words and phrases can increase the number of detailed visuals as children read, listen, and study. For example, here's how the *Amplified Bible* translates Psalm 1:1–2: "Blessed (happy, fortunate, prosperous, and enviable) is the man who walks *and* lives not in the counsel of the ungodly [following their advice, their plans and purposes], nor stands [submissive and inactive] in the path where sinners walk, nor sits down [to relax and rest] where the scornful [and the mockers] gather. But his delight *and* desire are in the law of the Lord, and on His law (the precepts, the instructions, the teachings of God) he habitually meditates (ponders and studies) by day and by night."

These children may also benefit from describing and/or drawing what they see when praying and worshiping. Giving credence to their minds' visuals is very honoring and will help them trust God. This is also a key when doing family devotions and when they study the Bible on their own. You can ask them, *"What did you see as I read that passage?"* This may help more than traditional questions like, *"What did you learn?"* and *"What did Jesus do first when arriving at the well?"* When studying, if children see Jesus feeding the five thousand (Mark 6:34–44) or healing Lazarus (John 11:1–44), their interest and faith may grow. (I was tempted to put the word *see* from the previous sentence in quotation marks. This would have indicated that they didn't really see Jesus. But I couldn't do this because it diminishes their reality. Many picture-smart children really *do* see Jesus—in their minds!)

If you're not very picture smart, it might surprise you to learn that the physical space picture-smart children use for their quiet times may be important to them. They might be distracted without the right visual atmosphere. They might want the area lit a certain way or decorated with a particular color. It's also relevant to consider the visual atmosphere where you typically hold family devotions and discussions.

These children may also want their church sanctuary and youth area to include elements of art and design. A number of years ago, I taught adults about multiple intelligences in a large sanctuary. It had tall, empty side walls with colors a few described as "dull." About half the audience indicated that the lack of beauty was distracting and troublesome to them. I imagine many children would have told me the same thing.

CHARACTER:
BE SMART WITH YOUR PICTURE SMART

Seeing beyond the Surface

Picture-smart children need to guard their eyes. They can sin by looking at what they shouldn't. They might also tend to judge people and things based only on appearance. This "judging a book by its cover" isn't God's way; 1 Samuel 16:7 states God looks at the heart. Another potential trap: Because their visual strengths allow them to see details, they may become critical and negative, eager to point out visual mistakes in someone's wardrobe, decorating, or school project. Consistently show them positive examples so they'll begin looking for them, too.

Depending on other factors, some picture-smart children

might tend to put their trust in their ability to look "just right." Or, some of their athletic skill may be due to picture-smart strengths and it can be easy to brag on that. They might develop gaming strengths. They might remember their scores, compare them to others, and place some of their security in beating their friends. Our security firmly rests in God who made us just the way we are.

These children may also study irrelevant things with their eyes. For example, if a history teacher's sweater has an unusual design, her picture-smart students may analyze it instead of listen to her. Children have told me about spots on shirts, crooked pictures in the kitchen, and dead flowers on tables interfering with their ability to concentrate. It's not easy for them to turn off their eyes. Self-control and self-respect are essential.

Let's Play!

Play *Telestrations*: Picture the "Telephone Game" using drawings instead of whispering something into your neighbor's ear. Lots of laughter.

Play *Pictionary*: Make quick sketches that others will hopefully guess correctly. Junior version available.

I AM MUSIC SMART:
I THINK WITH RHYTHMS
AND MELODIES

If intelligences were based on interest alone, it would be safe to say that today's children may be the most music-smart generation ever. Because music has always been readily accessible, this generation highly values it. They enjoy it. They prioritize it. They know it. Because of the quantity and variety of music on iTunes (invention of the year in 2003), make-your-own-radio-station sites like Spotify, bands on YouTube, and competition television shows involving music, they can know a variety of musical groups and styles. But when considering intelligences, ability must be factored in.

Does interest always foster talent? No. Here's a key question to consider: If my children indicate sincere interest, am I available to help with decision-making that results in ability gains?

MUSIC SMART:
THE SONG INSIDE YOUR CHILD

Music-smart children think with rhythms and melodies. When they're excited, they make music. They need to be able to express themselves musically. They get joy from being lost in music and accomplishing or exceeding their goal. Sound and music are their powers.

Many music-smart children don't just think with music in the traditional sense. They also find rhythms and melodies in the world around them to think with. American composer George Gershwin once said, "I frequently hear music in the heart of noise."[1] He reported getting many of his best musical ideas from the sounds of the city and your music-smart children might, too. Car windows going up and down, basketballs dribbled in the driveway accompanied by children's laughter, skateboards on the sidewalks, and babies crying in the kitchen.

Hearing music and sounds aren't all that music-smart children do. They also make noise. While listening to the above environmental sounds, if your son is inspired to drum along with his fingers or hum a tune, he's more music smart than his sister who listens but doesn't create. And, they're both more music smart than their sibling who doesn't even hear the sounds outside or in the room next door. You're more music smart than all of them if you actually go to your piano or guitar and compose and write down a little jingle triggered by the sounds you hear. Remember, every intelligence has a hierarchy of smartness.

You'll know when your music-smart children are excited because you'll usually hear or see the music inside of them. They may tap their fingers or feet to a particular beat or their whole body may shake, rattle, or roll to their internal song. They may spontaneously hum, whistle, or sing because of what's going on in their heart and head. Frequent reprimands to "Stop that noise!" or "Be quiet!" can paralyze this intelligence. Of course, so can ignoring or harshly critiquing their musical practices and performances.

Almost from the time my nieces could talk, they could sing. They responded frequently to life through song. They still do. If Betsy or Katie hears a word, phrase, or Bible verse that reminds her of a song, she will often begin singing. Soon her sister, brother, and parents join in. No wonder we sometimes refer to them as the "Von Koch Family Singers."

When music smart is a strength, children will do more than enjoy it. They may be able to sing in tune and/or play one or more instruments. Their musical ear will help them know if their violin is tuned correctly or if they're playing their trumpet at the right volume. They may want to participate in choir, orchestra, band, or musical theater. They might get involved in marching band, pep band, and/or pit orchestra. They might sing or play in ensembles to bless residents of nursing homes and in groups at church. They could travel internationally as part of a cultural exchange.

Music-smart children may enjoy different musical styles and may be able to distinguish among them and composers. Within the first few measures, these children can tell which of their favorite artists composed and is singing the piece. They begin to know their styles. If they're familiar with classical music, they may know if a symphony is by Brahms or Bach.

Relief and optimism are powerful outcomes of understanding these smarts.

I discovered an interesting and vital intelligence combination when in different Asian countries to support missionary families. Some of these missionaries had struggled to learn the language of the people they wanted to serve even though they're very word smart. Why? Because the language is tonal. Though they have word-smart strengths, some of them lack the music-smart ability to hear or create the fine differences in pitch and intonation required to express different meanings of words and phrases in a tonal language. The opposite implication is also clear. Children and adults who are music smart and word smart may have a special ability to learn tonal foreign languages.

I'll never forget watching some of the adults as they learned about these eight great smarts. They were listening as parents wanting to help their children and then the look on their faces changed. Some cried at a place in my teaching when tears don't typically flow. (Discoveries about past lies and new truths often result in tears.

Relief and optimism are powerful outcomes of understanding these smarts. I'm so glad you're reading this and open to discovering new truths for you *and* your children!)

Couples approached me to express amazement and gratitude and then I understood their reactions and tears. They found out they're not dumb even though the Asian language had been so hard to master. No. They're just not smart in a way that would have been very helpful. I know of at least a few families who chose to serve God in different regions because of what they learned. Victory!

LEARNING MATTERS: A SMART FOR LIFE

This smart is not essential for school success. That doesn't mean it's unimportant. It might be among the most important for your son or daughter. Having interest and ability in music might be what keeps them in school when the core courses of science, history, English, and math challenge and frustrate them. I've met students tempted to drop out except they were enjoying band too much.

This also might be the smart that enriches their lives after they graduate. Music stimulates emotion and can move people to action.

Once stretched, a smart never goes back to its original size.

You know what matters in the long run? Life success. Yes! I tell parents and educators all the time that the purpose of school is not to prepare children for more school. It's to prepare them for life. A good life. A fulfilling life. A life of meaning and contribution. So even the two school smarts—word and logic—are for more than school. Do you agree? Raise your children to agree and their lives will be more complete.

Because of your choice or theirs, some children will take piano lessons for just a year or two. They might ask to stop taking lessons or their disinterest may make it obvious that they should. Even if they quit, the time and money hasn't been wasted. Trust that the investment has awakened and broadened their music smart. Plus, there's no way their character hasn't been positively affected by taking lessons so this is another great benefit.

Other children will continue taking lessons, join musical groups, and stay invested into their adult years. For example, my brother is in his sixties and regularly plays his trumpet in a church orchestra. He and his wife also play in a handbell choir. Their daughter, Betsy, took piano and trumpet lessons for years and was very involved with music through high school. She then took a break, but recently purchased a used piano for her home and enjoys playing to relax. Once stretched, a smart never goes back to its original size. She has remembered her favorite songs.

Strengthening Music Smart: Prioritizing Piano—and More
If you want to further develop your children's music-smartness, have music playing often in the background. You can attend concerts with them, listen to and talk about a variety of musical styles, talk

with musicians, and encourage your children to learn an instrument and/or sing in a choir. Point out music and sounds in the environment, too.

Even if you have no skill, your children can be skilled.

Friends of mine have four teenage daughters who all play the piano beautifully. Their oldest is majoring in piano performance in college. Their second has a definite bent toward composition. I love what these friends did to awaken and increase their daughters' interest in piano and their ability, too.

Tracie, their mom, says she doesn't have any musical ability at all, but she wanted her girls to have some. Richard, their dad, played the piano growing up and knows the benefit and joy it can bring. They decided to homeschool the girls and to prioritize piano as a part of their day.

In addition to providing for private lessons and celebrating the girls' progress at recitals, guess what Tracie did? She purchased and continues to purchase movie soundtracks for her girls. Because the music in the movie is used to help tell a story, they have found this music to be rich and emotionally fulfilling. I listened as their youngest told me about her favorite soundtrack. I wish you could have seen her glow and speak with confidence.

Tracie's message is important. Even if you have no skill, your children can be skilled. Remember what I wrote about in chapter 1. Children's smarts are a combination of nature and nurture. These girls clearly enjoy playing the piano and are gifted. But if their mother had assumed that because she was not musical they wouldn't be either, their music smarts never would have been awakened. I'll repeat this: Even if you have no skill, your children can be skilled.

Learning Struggles: The Danger of Distraction

Not having music smart as a strength might make memorization of vocabulary words, math facts, and the like more challenging because music can build those muscles. And, if children have no strong interests that connect them to courses and extras like music, art, or athletics, school won't be as enjoyable in general. This, alone, is a valid reason to help children discover music and then develop their abilities.

Music-smart students need to be self-disciplined so they don't get distracted by music while studying. Because they enjoy it, they may listen while reading and working on assignments. But it's possible that more of their attention will be diverted to the music than to what they're reading or writing. It can, therefore, take them much longer to do the work and it may not be done as well. Children tell me they don't plan to analyze music that's playing in the background, but they can't help themselves.

My sister-in-law, Debbie, is like that. She can't have music playing during her quiet time because she'll think about the last time she heard the same song, she'll wonder if what she just heard was a bassoon or an oboe, and she'll begin humming along. But if she's in her home cooking or cleaning, music will be playing.

Some of us aren't that consistent. Sometimes, while writing this book, I've listened to music. At other times, I haven't. I'm very music smart—I actually chose Purdue University so I could march in their amazing band. Sometimes music works for me because silence is distracting. At other times, I need quiet. Let's help children discern what works for them.

Too many children have pods in their ears at all times, assuming they need music. But maybe they don't. Maybe they'd be more relaxed, respectful, and efficient without it. We'll have to help them set up "experiments" to see what's best. They also might need strength and assistance to stand up to peers who think music is everything.

Teaching the Music-Smart Child: "MISSISSIPPI" and More

Music can add to learning in many areas.[2] In history, lessons about the Civil War can be enhanced by playing music from that era. In art, you can play energizing music when you want children to draw quickly and spontaneously. You can also use music to create a certain mood that helps children be more creative. This will help all children because music will activate an intelligence that otherwise might have been ignored in that context. When your child learns and studies with two or more intelligences, he or she will probably do better than if only one is used. You do need to remember, however, that some children can't concentrate with music playing in the background. Therefore, don't play music all the time.

I know of a world geography teacher who teaches the names and spellings of many countries of the world with rhymes and jingles she makes up. I've heard her students sing some of them, and they're very effective. Years later, because many of these young people can still remember the rhymes, they can remember the countries of the world. Another friend, a math teacher, uses a song to help students learn the quadratic formula. Many of us have learned the order of the books of the Bible through a song.

During my assemblies and chapels, when I ask children and teens to say the ABCs, they frequently sing them. They don't *intend* to sing them. They don't *decide* to sing them. The "ABC Song" just comes out. Many laugh. Most of them enjoy finishing the song!

A similar thing occurs when I ask children to spell "Mississippi." They spell it with the rhythm that is the same everywhere I go. It's virtually impossible to spell this word without the rhythm. (Go ahead and try it.) The use of music improves long-term memory. Therefore, we'll probably never forget the ABCs or how to spell "Mississippi."

No matter their age, children can benefit by putting to music things they must memorize. They might be able to use the same rhythm as "Mississippi" and/or the melody of the "ABC Song." They can make up their own rhythm or melody. I often recommend that older children replace the lyrics from their favorite song with what they need to remember. For example, this can work with the order of events for their history test, abbreviations for their science class, and words and definitions for health. They can sing this new "song" aloud while at home and in their mind while taking a test in school.

Young children can use the power of sound and music when learning. For instance, if your son struggles to remember the silent "h" in "whisper," you can have him whisper the "h" when saying the letters aloud as you help him study. He would say all the other letters with normal volume. This unique way to emphasize the "h" can help your son remember it's there.

Clapping can work, too. When studying addition facts, young children can clap and recite the problem orally: 2 (clap, clap) + 2 (clap, clap) = 4 (clap, clap, clap, clap). This nicely combines several intelligences. They're using word smart because they're talking and listening, logic smart because they're adding, music smart because there will be a rhythm to their clapping, and body smart because they're moving. Although it can be overwhelming it you overdo it, sometimes the more intelligences, the better!

WHEN THEY GROW UP:
CAREERS AND EDUCATION

Music-smart children can use their abilities and interests in several careers. They can become music therapists, worship pastors, music teachers, composers, conductors, music arrangers, music producers, soloists, and owners of music/instrument stores. They can become jingle writers, advertisers, disc jockeys, and piano tuners. They can help to design websites and videos that use music effectively.

Perhaps your music-smart child would enjoy a career related to movies, television shows, or theater. He or she could be a music editor, sound designer, or sound engineer.

RELATIONSHIPS

How Music Can Bond Us

Because music is important to this generation, children who aren't interested may struggle relationally. Their friends may be talking about songs and groups they've never heard of. They may not enjoy doing the same things in their spare time. This can make it harder to get to know each other and remain close friends over time. These are valid reasons to awaken and develop children's music-smart abilities.

Some music-smart children tell me that just taking time for friendship is difficult because of the amount of practice and number of rehearsals they must attend. For these reasons, many music-smart children find their friends within their music groups. I sure did.

Music serves as a powerful bonding agent, providing something to talk about and an emotional experience to share. Music can be enjoyed and experienced for a lifetime, as evidenced by my mom. At eighty years old, she and friends had season tickets for the Milwaukee Symphony Orchestra. Music was important to my mom when she was a little girl learning to play the piano and all the way to the end of her life when I played CDs for her at the hospice center.

Music has certainly been a bonding agent in my family. In addition to Dave and me, my four cousins on my mom's side are also music smart. We were in junior high and high school band and orchestra together. We formed a unique ensemble when we played for our grandparents' fiftieth and sixty-fifth wedding anniversary parties. Dave was on the trumpet, Terry on sax, Jane on French horn, I was on the viola, Ann played the clarinet, and Nancy played the flute. When my brother married Debbie, she joined us on the piano. Our junior high band director was nice enough to arrange some of my grandparents' favorite songs for our rather strange combination of instruments. We actually sounded quite good. I can close my eyes and see and hear us playing "The Waltz You Saved for Me." Music creates vivid memories and emotions that last. I don't just remember the music. I remember my family and the love we all had for our grandparents and the love they had for us.

When I'm with my sister-in-law, who is a music teacher by profession and also very word smart, and we hear the word "sisters" spoken just right, we jump into "Sisters, sisters, there were never such devoted sisters" from a song in the movie *White Christmas*. It just takes that one word.

At the zoo once, when overhearing a mom ask her children if they'd like to go into the birdhouse to feed the birds, one observer began to sing "Feed the Birds" from the movie *Mary Poppins*. It wasn't long before a group of us joined in. Then, of course, we all enjoyed a good laugh.

Do you have the same abilities? It means you're music smart! Singing songs you're reminded of can add to your joy and strengthen relationships as you discover something you have in common. Mostly, though, it's just fun!

RELATING TO PARENTS:
THE IMPORTANCE OF INVESTING

When you're truly open to hearing why your daughter likes the music she likes, she will trust you more. Ask to listen to her music with her. Ask her why certain songs speak to her. You might be pleasantly surprised at what she gains from lyrics you think are shallow. Of course, you'll definitely have standards as to lyrics and volume and maybe style and draw the line at what music she's allowed to listen to. She may never thank you, but that shouldn't matter.

If you do have your child learn an instrument or join a choir, support both the practices and performances. I'm often asked what I think my parents did right to raise two well-rounded children with PhDs who are devoted to God, involved in church, healthy, and generally doing very well in life. One of the first answers I provide is that my parents were genuinely interested in what we did. They enjoyed what we pursued, they had confidence in us, and they communicated that confidence. Dave and I knew we could accomplish just about anything!

Our parents didn't just attend our concerts and recitals, clapping and taking pictures. They made sure our grandparents and great-aunts knew about them so they could attend, too. They paid for and took us to-and-from many private lessons. Many! They sacrificed and provided for us. (Ask me about my favorite Christmas gift sometime.) To encourage us to practice, they sat in the living room with us at times. They provided helpful feedback. They cared about our efforts that resulted in our performances. I believe this is essential. Invest in the process that leads your children to the product they can achieve. Read that sentence again. It's that important. And it's not just true of music.

SPIRITUAL GROWTH

Praise, Worship . . . and Whistling

You could encourage your music-smart child to find music to play occasionally in the background during family devotions. Better yet, share the devotional topic in advance (e.g., God's strength or bearing one another's burdens) and ask him or her to find a song to play at the end.

It won't surprise you to know that most music-smart children will connect with God through praise and worship. Whether they're self-smart or people smart may influence whether they find individual or corporate worship most fulfilling.

Some music-smart children will study and reflect upon the lyrics of traditional hymns and modern praise choruses. Those who have word-smart strengths may enjoy finding Scripture that supports the songs. Music-smart children may enjoy learning about the lives of composers and lyricists and the circumstances that caused them to compose the songs and pen the lyrics we sing.

Music-smart children will want their church to have quality musical worship. Especially if they're musically and spiritually mature, they'll want members of worship teams to be talented, but also to be more concerned with leading others into worship than with their own performances. They might prefer to have a variety of musical styles represented. The quality of music during youth and children's events is an important consideration, too.

Because I'm music smart, God will often meet my needs through song. He did this with "How Great Thou Art" when I was twelve years old. I played it as a viola solo during a worship service. I practiced hard and remember being inspired when it dawned on me that the lyrics were true. God used this song and performance opportunity to awaken in me a desire to get to know Him. I'm grateful!

I can't tell you how many times God has directed my church's worship leader to have us sing a song I needed to sing. Also, the right song often comes up on the car radio at the right time. This is how God works with music-smart people. Teach this to your music-smart children so they understand it's not a coincidence when God meets a need or answers a prayer with a song.

I sometimes whistle. It's completely spontaneous. I don't think, *I haven't whistled in a while. I think I'll whistle!* I just hear myself whistling. I might be in a hotel room, my office, or walking into a grocery store. I learned a long time ago that whistling is my music-smart self responding to my internal peace. When I realize I'm whistling, it's God saying, "Kathy, pay attention to your peace." It's a beautiful thing! Teach your children to pay attention to these types of occurrences. They need to see God active in their lives!

CHARACTER:
BE SMART WITH YOUR MUSIC SMART

Keeping a Healthy Perspective

Music-smart children may make noise when they shouldn't, by tapping feet or fingers, by humming or singing; and they may play their music louder than others prefer. If they're asked to stop and don't, this disobedience can negatively influence relationships with family members, friends, and teachers.

Some children may cross over from enjoying music to actually idolizing music and/or artists they enjoy. Listen closely to your children. The more you hear them talk about "loving" their music, the more concerned you might want to be. Asking them how much time they spend with God versus how much time they listen to music might be an effective way to begin the conversation. You can also ask if any of their music doesn't edify God, and what they should do if it doesn't.

If they sing and/or play well enough to be part of a performing group, their motivation matters. Do they want to play or sing without error so they look good or do they want God to look good? Do they whine about practicing and complain to their parents during the week, but then act on a Sunday morning as if they're thrilled to lead people into God's presence? Do they glorify Him during the service, but not while they practice? Gently remind them that God pays attention to it all.

Music-smart children may fall into pride in their musical skills, performances, and understandings. If they participate on worship teams, they may believe their public service to God is more important than their private worship or the service some people do behind the scenes. This is another type of pride. In addition, some music-smart children may look down on others who don't participate in or enjoy music.

There's also the tendency to perfectionism. Because a piece is meant to be played a certain defined way, they may be very hard on themselves when they make a mistake. Forgiving themselves may be hard. Paralysis can set in when others are hard on them. High standards that are realistic are appropriate. So is allowing for mistakes and growth. Absolutely![3] Music can be one of the best ways for children to learn a proper perspective of self-discipline, practice, the reality of mistakes, and the proper place and time to want and expect perfection. They can also learn about the joy that comes with both practice and excellence. Character and discipline grow through learning, practice, and performing.

Well, that's four of the eight smarts. How are you doing? Encouraged? Optimistic? Curious about the next four? Great! Are you sharing what you're learning directly with your children? I hope so, because I know from lots of experience that most children will be interested and encouraged. Also, remember that we created the online interactive tool for you so you can identify which intelligences are strengths and which aren't. You may enjoy using that, as will your children. You can find it here: www.8GreatSmarts.com.

Let's Play!

Play *Cranium*: Answer trivia questions, create art, hum, act out clues, and use your vocabulary skills to win. Relevant to many smarts.

Play *Encore*: Draw a card with a word on it and sing at least six words of a song with that word in it. Judges memory, not musical ability.

I AM BODY SMART: I THINK WITH MOVEMENT AND TOUCH

At the beginning of chapter 5, I shared part of a letter from Kristin, my former university student who was now teaching dance. She wrote me after learning that she was both picture smart and body smart. If you remember, God used the seminar to replace lies and doubts with truths and confidence. Here's more of Kristin's story.

When she was a senior in high school, her guidance counselor tried to discourage her from going to college, declaring she would never graduate. She enrolled in a nearby college anyway because her parents wanted her to. In her letter to me, she wrote, "I didn't expect to graduate. After all, college was for smart kids who like to study."

Kristin chose to major in theater because of positive high

school experiences. Drama combined both her picture- and body-smart strengths, although she didn't call them that. She was able to picture how selected costumes and sets would enhance a particular play. She was able to use her body to effectively mimic a tottering elderly lady or to portray a tired middle-aged woman when those were her assigned parts. I thank God for leading Kristin to college and to this major and am glad she didn't follow her guidance counselor's advice. Without her parents' support, I'm afraid she might have.

Kristin graduated from college with a higher GPA than she ever had in high school. Not only that, she also earned a master's degree, graduating magna cum laude. She included this in her letter to me: "I was just short of bursting at the seams with joy and pride. It was so rewarding to obtain a second degree, with honors—especially after being told that I would drop out."

Here's what she wrote next:

I've had a busy thirteen years since graduating from high school. I feel satisfied with the path my career has taken me: performing in four summer seasons across the nation, working within Walt Disney World's creative costuming department, choreographing professionally in four different states, and touring the nation and Canada as a puppeteer and dancer with an internationally acclaimed performance group . . . But, up until [attending your workshop], I never would have used the word "smart" to describe myself. I didn't know that the reason I am good at theater is because I am smart . . .

Students outside my field in college constantly asked, "Are you taking any real classes this semester?" It made me realize the rest of the world thought that what I'm best at took no brainpower. So it became easy to believe that while some people are smart, others are talented, and it became even easier for me to turn green with envy when I saw someone who appeared to be both . . .

I can't tell you how freeing it is to find out that I am smart, that my abilities come from a God-wired part of my brain!

I fear for kids like me, not because of how they are smart but because of how people respond to how they are smart.

Perhaps you can relate to Kristin's statements because of your own past or your child's strengths or struggles. If not, I imagine you know someone who shares similar experiences to Kristin's. The word *smart* is empowering. I encourage you to use it! The following information will help you know when to do just that.

BODY SMART:
THE POWER OF MOTION

Body-smart children think with movement and touch. When they're excited, they move more. They need freedom and sometimes lots of space to move productively. They get joy from accomplishing or surpassing their physical goal so everything comes together perfectly. Motion is their power.

When being body smart, children learn and think with their entire bodies. Their hands are busy "talking," building, writing, touching, twisting hair, playing, etc. Their feet are busy tapping, shifting in place, or walking. Body-smart children are often moving—sometimes purposefully and intentionally, sometimes not. This is because when body-smart children are excited, they can't help but move. Being in motion is like breathing to body-smart children.

Body-smart children are usually good at large-motor tasks because they can control their entire body. Therefore, they may enjoy and be successful at physical pursuits like hiking, sports, dancing, acting, camping, and/or playing musical instruments. How might being body smart influence the choice of which instrument to play? These children might prefer drums, trombone (which is dependent upon remembering and feeling how far out to pull the slide), and string bass (which they can stand and play and requires full-body posture and balance). Make sense? Yet, we can't put children in boxes. My niece Katie, who is so body smart she earned a college soccer scholarship, chose to play the flute. She liked the tone.

Often body-smart children can easily execute small-motor tasks. Their eye-hand coordination allows them to handle objects carefully and to master skills using the finer muscles of their fingers and hands. Small-muscle movements are needed for such skills as sewing, carpentry, model building, cooking, handwriting, and typing. And, the playing of Katie's flute. These are also the children who may like and win certain online and computer games because of how quickly their fingers can react to things on the screen.

It's possible to have strengths in large-motor areas but not in small-motor skills, or vice versa. Understandably, children with abilities and interests in both are more body smart than children with strengths in just one area. If it's hard to identify strengths with either large-motor or small-motor tasks, maybe body smart hasn't been fully awakened yet. If this is true for one or more of your children, I trust you'll make it a priority to awaken it soon. Just get out of the house and go to the park.

My body smart was awakened because of a wise decision my parents made when I was about six years old. Until then, I had obviously used my body to walk, run, play, color, cut, etc. Nevertheless, not unlike many children, I was somewhat clumsy. My parents enrolled me in dance class and God used tap and ballet instruction to establish connections between my brain and my body. I'm grateful my parents didn't just assume I was destined to be clumsy. Rather, they were solution-focused problem solvers and I overcame my clumsiness.

After hearing me teach about this intelligence, many children share that they never knew moving well was a way of being smart. I find great joy in helping these children redefine themselves as "smart." Although this intelligence doesn't get the same respect in school that word and logic smart do, children with large-motor and/or small-motor skills *are* smart. They're not just athletic, good sculptors, children with neat handwriting, or good at putting a worm on a hook. They're smart because they do those things well. One of my fond memories is of a student who came up after a high school assembly and declared: "I'm not a dumb jock. I'm a smart one!"

Many children suspected of having Attention Deficit Hyperactivity Disorder (ADHD) may be body smart, not ADHD.

Body-smart children can demonstrate this intelligence in many ways. They can learn sign language so they can interpret for the deaf during church services and conferences. Or they might form or join a church drama or dance team. Puppetry and clowning come easily to many body-smart children. They may enjoy using these skills to present evangelistic programs for younger boys and girls.

Athletes can demonstrate Christlikeness on church-sponsored or school teams, or when helping to coach younger children's sports teams. They can also use sports as a platform for evangelism. My niece Katie traveled to Northern Ireland to play soccer when she was in high school and to South Africa with her college team.

On these mission trips, she told athletes on the other teams, *"I play for Christ. That's why I play. Why do you play?"*

Perhaps you've already thought of this: Many children suspected of having Attention Deficit Hyperactivity Disorder (ADHD) may be body smart, *not* ADHD. This disorder and the smart have things in common—moving and learning by touching and direct experiences—so one can be disguised as the other. Many children who have been properly assessed and diagnosed as having ADHD may *also* be body smart. If this is your son or daughter, I encourage you to choose to see his or her physical energy and the ways he or she embraces life through touch and action as strengths. Although proper medication is sometimes appropriate, we must be careful to not medicate out of these children the greatest channel God has given them through which to experience life. I tell children that I'm not so concerned with whether they have ADHD or not but that they choose to respect others and be self-controlled regardless.

Another contrast to be aware of is between body-smart children and kinesthetic learners. Just as auditory learners aren't necessarily word smart and visual learners may or may not be picture smart, some children who appear to be body smart may be kinesthetic learners instead. These children *remember* what they do. Body-smart children *think with* their movements and touch. It's possible to be one, both, or to have strengths in neither.

I'm so body smart that when I'm in the fitness center working out with my trainer, Linda, I'll regularly think of ideas related to a blog I'm writing or a book chapter I'm finishing. I may think of the next video to film or something to talk with a member of my staff about. I'm moving and that causes thinking—and the thinking isn't even related to the movement. I might be biking, lifting free weights, or on a machine working my back. But these movements somehow stimulate thought. When my workout is over, I quickly capture the ideas with a note in my phone or by writing them down.

The kinesthetic part of me comes in handy at the gym, too. It's what allows my muscles to remember doing an exercise in the past. Just this week, Linda had me do a challenging exercise for the shoulders. We do three different reps and the first time at that station, finishing the twelve reps was very challenging. I almost didn't complete the last two. But a few minutes later, after two other exercises in between, I returned to that station and did the twelve reps without as much trouble. The third time was easier still. Why? My muscles remembered what they were supposed to do.

If your child is a kinesthetic learner, that's great. He or she will remember things by doing them. Writing the word will be more effective than just looking at the word on the page. If he runs the basketball play at practice rather than just hearing it described, he will more likely remember how to execute it during the game. They move productively *to remember*. Body-smart children move productively *and* not productively *to think*.

LEARNING MATTERS:
SPORTS, DRAMA, AND MORE

If you divide body smart into different elements, it can be easier to see what hasn't been awakened yet and what can be strengthened. How are you and your child doing in areas such as balance, coordination, flexibility, strength, endurance, reflexes, dexterity, and hand-eye coordination?

The value of this smart is similar to that of music smart. It can definitely enhance a child's life and provide motivation for school and great friendships. In most cases, it's not terribly relevant to how children will do in the core academic classes. Fit children do sleep better than others and may have better attention spans. It's relevant in these ways. It is, of course, relevant to physical education classes and certain units in art classes. For instance, these children may do better sculpting with clay while picture-smart children may do better painting with acrylics. This also explains why they may be better at creating a model of the solar system in a science class than students who earn As on tests. If they're also strong in picture-smart abilities, it will be even easier and more enjoyable for them.

If your son wants to play soccer well, a particular team or league might be necessary. Just as with private music lessons and recitals, you have to decide what's best for your son and healthiest for your family. Exposing children to things is how talents and passions are discovered. Playing some soccer is fine. Having all your children on competition teams all season long may not be necessary or appropriate. Remember to acknowledge each child's individuality. Just because one plays soccer doesn't mean all your children need to.[1]

I'm writing about sports, but the same thing is true for drama, crafts, and other things body-smart children gravitate toward. Considering balance and the whole family are appropriate. The oldest daughter of friends of mine is very involved in drama. This means many rehearsals and performances and it all keeps Nicole especially busy driving her to and from it all. Nicole and Eric have chosen to prioritize this for Audrey because it has allowed her to discover a healthy identity and belonging apart from her four younger siblings.

Strengthening Body Smart: Get Outside!

As with the other smarts, your nurture combined with a child's nature will determine whether body smart will be a strength. Choosing to support your child's interests increases the likelihood that abilities will develop. Being physically active yourself, prioritizing time for large-motor and small-motor body-smart activities, and involving your child in different activities will be key.

Putting down electronic devices and going outside can strengthen this smart. You can roll in the grass, shoot hoops, play catch, and walk or bike around the neighborhood. You can make houses with a deck of cards, put glue on tiny items as you make crafts together, and have your child stir the stew.

Chores can awaken and strengthen this smart, too. Your child can sweep the garage, wash the car, and help you add rocks to the rock garden. Your child can wash spiderwebs and dirt from the front door and shingles, load the dishwasher, and fold the laundry. Sometimes the very chores we don't think to assign to our children because they'll be hard are the very ones they should do. Right?

Learning Struggles: Your Child and School

"School is horrible. That is all, carry on." When writing this chapter, I noticed this post on Facebook. I've heard thousands of versions of the "school is horrible" comment and they often come from children and young adults who are body smart and aren't very word smart and logic smart. It saddens and concerns me that many body-smart children have negative school experiences. If your child's needs have been met by his or her teachers, I hope you affirm and thank them regularly. If you're your child's teacher doing this well, thank you!

Remember Kristin's statement in the letter she sent me? "I didn't know that the reason I am good at theater is because I am smart." Substitute "theater" with whatever body-smart ability is appropriate for your child. Building a complicated diorama? Making layups with both hands? Karate? Children must understand they can use their bodies and hands well because they are smart.

When these children are allowed to move purposefully, they'll have less need to move in disruptive ways. This will help them feel smart and be smart with their smarts. Expecting body-smart children to sit still and keep their hands still for long stretches isn't fair or realistic. This expectation and the constant commands to "Sit still!" and "Put that down!" that often accompany it can discourage children and paralyze their body smart.

The structure of school may be the issue that is the hardest for body-smart children to cope with and overcome. Talk about, model, and teach children to have self-respect, self-control, and respect for others. These affect learning and relationships. These affect life.

Teaching Your Child: Purposeful Movement

Anytime you can work purposeful movement and/or productive touch into lessons, especially body-smart children will benefit. Other children will benefit, too, because your assignments will activate a smart they won't naturally use on their own. This can increase motivation and learning.

Young children can march to their spelling words, taking one step for each letter. The teacher can lead them during school and children can march when practicing at home. If they do this with the word "Texas" at home and then forget the middle letter when taking their spelling test, they can silently march with their big toes under their desks. This "marching" will help them recall the letter "x." Once this method has been used, if children determine it helps them, they can use it at home even when the teacher doesn't use it at school. This is why one of the most important conversations parents can have with children is about *why* they did well or didn't do well on quizzes, tests, and assignments.[2]

Recently, I met with a mom and her second-grade daughter, Pamela, who was struggling with phonics, spelling, and other word-smart tasks. Because Pamela is body smart and good with her hands, I suggested that she practice her words and phonics patterns using skywriting. This meant she would "write" her letters and words as large as she could make them in the air with her hand, as if she was holding her pencil. Skywriting also works well when learning chemical formulas, an explorer's name, or a cursive letter. As an alternative to skywriting, I explained that Pamela could use large pieces of chalk on the driveway, wet sponges on chalkboards, and markers on whiteboards.

Because skywriting involves muscles in the fingers, arm, shoulder, and back, it's better for body-smart children than

It helps if you never proclaim, "You can't sit still!"

simply writing on paper. Muscle movement helps body-smart children think. I recommend that children also say what they're writing, because then they'll be using two more components of word smart—speaking and listening—along with the word-smart skill of writing and the body's large-motor actions.

Body-smart children benefit from having clipboards available for their use. They'll have the freedom to pace and study, go sit outside for a while, and sprawl out on the floor in the den where they can freely kick their legs in the air. They may also benefit from reading and studying in rocking chairs and beanbag chairs because these chairs provide the freedom to move. Even "studying" while emptying the dishwasher, cutting the grass, and washing the car may help. Of course, they won't be holding a textbook, but they can rehearse a poem they're memorizing, verbalize the order of events they're studying for their history test, or think through a paper they're writing.

Have you ever had a great idea while driving, putting groceries away, or walking upstairs like I have when I'm moving at my fitness club? If you have, that's your body smart at work. This is precisely why these children should not be expected or required to always sit still. It's counterproductive and unrealistic for the way God wired them. When it's essential they sit still because of the activity they're completing or there are other children present, they must learn to use their self-control to be obedient. Like everything, it's a choice.

It helps if you never proclaim "You can't sit still!" Also, you don't want your son to overhear you telling someone: "He moves constantly and never sits still!!" After hearing and overhearing things like this, your son may not be very confident when you ask him to sit still at grandma's or because his sister is working hard and can't be distracted. We must speak the truth. For instance: "Sitting still for long periods of time challenges him." "He's very body smart so sitting still and being quiet isn't easy." "He's using more self-control and sitting still longer than he used to. I'm very proud of him."

Learning through drama and role-play can also be effective. It doesn't have to be involved and complicated. When teaching children about Daniel and faith, I remind them of Daniel's strong faith in his great God and that he was in a den with lions. I explain that on the count of three I want them to stand as they think Daniel stood among the lions. Some just stand casually, some take a worship posture, and others kneel or position their hands to pray. It's impressive! As the lesson continues, I ask them how *they* think *they* would have stood if *they* had been in the den. I then count to three and have them picture in their minds what they would have done. Their facial expressions tell me that they saw themselves and are thinking about their stance.

Because body-smart children think and learn by touching, it makes sense to use manipulatives. Bending colorful pipe cleaners into letters and numbers may work well. So might using magnetic letters on the refrigerator. Giving children relevant objects to explore and examine can be very motivational and instructive. Remember, they think with their hands, so actually handling an old beehive could do more for them than a ten-minute lecture about it.

Many of these ideas are used regularly by teachers of young

children, in part, because they don't expect their students to sit still for long periods. Often children's motivation and grades decline as they age because their body-smart strengths are honored only when they're young. I'm always enthusiastic when I meet teachers of older children who have worked to implement activities that help their body-smart students concentrate and learn. These teachers impress me because I know it's not always easy. If you're homeschooling, remember to always honor the way your children are created. If you send your children to school, you can help them study at home with their whole mind even if teachers don't use all the smarts.

WHEN THEY GROW UP:
CAREERS AND EDUCATION

Children who are very body smart will probably gravitate toward careers that rely on touch, hand-eye coordination, and/or large-motor movements. I'm glad Cari, my hairdresser, is body smart and cuts my hair and not my ear! I'm glad my fitness trainer is body smart. She can demonstrate what she wants me to do so I'm more confident. She spots me when I do exercises like "skull crushers" so I actually don't crush my skull. (The logic-smart part of me wants to know who names these things!)

Perhaps your child will enjoy these or any of the following vocations: mechanic, physical education teacher, orchestra conductor, carpenter, plumber, welder, truck driver, stunt person, physical therapist, surgeon, actor, seamstress, sports coach, or camp director.

RELATIONSHIPS:
PART OF THE TEAM

Belonging is a need every child has. Many body-smart children will meet this need through team sports. Typically, they relate well to other athletes and enjoy the camaraderie, especially if they are also people smart. They may also enjoy watching live and televised sporting events with friends and family members.

Body-smart children might also bond during shop class, as they work with peers to create wood toys for hospitalized children. Of course, the other activities they participate in, such as drama and art, will also strengthen their belonging.

It's also possible that body-smart children will be most accepted by other children who move frequently. I notice that those who move and touch a lot often have best friends who are just like them. This is because they bond, at times, through misbehavior. Ideally, they can learn to help each other and even hold each other accountable to make wise choices.

The almost constant motion of some body-smart children can distract and irritate others. For this reason, other children may not choose them as friends. How parents and teachers react to body-smart children and what they tell other children about them influences how strong their belonging will be. If non-body-smart children only see these children as troublemakers, they may choose to ignore them. This is unfortunate, because their high energy could be a blessing rather than an irritation.

RELATING TO PARENTS:
THE PHYSICAL CONNECTION

Body-smart children will trust you when you view their energy and need for action as positive qualities. In contrast, children will distance themselves from parents who are easily frustrated and who constantly tell them to sit down, sit still, and keep their hands to themselves.

Children pay attention to and trust parents who help them develop their body-smartness through lessons, practicing in the backyard, spending time on relevant activities, and by providing needed materials for their use. This is especially true when children and parents play a sport together and work together on projects, such as changing the oil in a car, building a pinewood derby car, and sweeping out the garage. I imagine there are many parents and children who can testify to bonds formed in the swimming pool or on the golf course. Children may talk more during these body-smart times and thus increase the quality of their belonging. Belonging and trust go hand in hand.

Considering body-smartness when disciplining and motivating

children means you will let children move respectfully during serious talks. Ask them to act out solutions rather than simply talking about them. Even practicing proper behavior—like walking in the kitchen rather than running—may help, as long as the practice isn't overdone or assigned in a demeaning way.

Remember these children learn through touch. Therefore, use touch-praise and touch-correction judiciously. When you want to compliment a child who is body smart, pat him on the back, tussle his hair, and make eye contact while you speak the affirmation. The same is true when you need to offer helpful correction. Gently touch your daughter's wrist when you talk with her about her need to put things down the first time you ask. Gently touch your son's forehead when you talk with him about his need to slow down and think more carefully about what he is doing. These physical connections may help your children remember your words.

SPIRITUAL GROWTH

A Moving Experience

Body-smart children may connect with God best when they move. Being physically involved during worship may be important to them. However, be careful not to judge whether someone is body smart based only on whether they sway, clap, or lift their hands during worship. One of my best friends is very body smart and yet very still as she worships God. She talks with her hands, is a former athlete, exercises regularly, and enjoys rocking chairs; but while worshiping, her body is often still.

Because body-smart children learn by doing and by experiencing things for themselves, the sacraments of Communion and baptism and practices like financial giving can be very important. You may want to attend baptism services, have children put money in the offering plate, and take advantage of Communion as a very important teaching time.

Family devotions will also be more effective when you plan something for these children to do. Anything that keeps their hands busy will help. Allow them to stand, pace, or wiggle in their chair. Using drama, action, and object lessons in shorter teaching times will help.

Just as picture-smart children need to learn to trust the pictures God gives them, body-smart children should be encouraged to trust their gut reactions and physical responses. They may talk about feeling certain they shouldn't go to a concert or that they should call their grandmother. They might also talk about "being moved" to do or say something.

Remember my illustration where I ask children to picture themselves standing as if they had been in the lions' den with Daniel? Numerous children have told me that's been a more effective way for them to judge the depth of their faith than anything else they've experienced.

CHARACTER:
BE SMART WITH YOUR BODY SMART
Learning to Respect Others

Children who are body smart might be tempted to use their bodies to hurt others and to get themselves into trouble. When young, they may express their frustrations and fears with their bodies, by punching, kicking, pinching, or biting. They might choose to shove their way to the front of the line just because they can. As they mature and learn language, you can teach them to use words to express themselves. And your training can help them be obedient and use their need for touch and movement in only positive ways. Absolutely! It can be challenging, but it's very possible.

I'm sad for how many body-smart children I meet who think of themselves as "bad" and "in trouble all the time." They need to be affirmed for who they are and taught and trained to use their bodies well and not just told to "stop that." Seriously! I wish you could overhear some conversations I've had with these children—young and old—who cry with me because they're so frustrated. Some are angry with God for the way He made them. That's not good! These are great kids!

I know it can be hard. Children with body-smart strengths will often drum their fingers, tap their feet, constantly play with something in their hands, or find another way to move somehow. Asking them

Intelligence strengths are no excuse for disobedience.

to stop is almost always only a temporary solution. Their body reacts to truth with movement, so they need to find ways to move that are respectful.

For instance, I teach body-smart children to drum their fingers on their thigh, under the table or their desk. Initially, it's not as satisfying as doing it on a table because it doesn't make noise, but they can choose to learn to be satisfied. Here's another example. When the movement or noise of their tapping foot is distracting to others, they can choose to tap their big toe to the beat in their mind. They can choose to learn to be satisfied by this smaller and silent movement. That's the key. We can all "choose to learn to be satisfied."

Intelligence strengths are no excuse for disobedience. Obedience is right. All children must learn to be smart with their smarts—using them to help and not hurt. When these children know they're smart because they move well, they may find the motivation and self-respect, self-control, and respect for others necessary to be positive, contributing members of groups.

Let's revisit one of Kristin's statements. She wrote, "There are lots of words I would use to describe myself. Accomplished—yes; successful—yes; assertive, driven, hardworking, talented, creative, determined, gifted, well-educated, and informed." Our children's success will always be a combination of their smarts and their character. Their nature and nurture. Their choices and ours. Always! The same is true for us.

Let's Play!

Play tag (or any outdoor game).

Play *Twister*: Give the spinner a whirl and follow the directions. Just try to keep from falling over!

I AM NATURE SMART:
I THINK WITH PATTERNS

My niece Betsy is definitely someone who can declare, *"I am nature smart!"* Her natural inclination toward animals means she was always comfortable around them. When she was very young and visited petting zoos, her parents report that she *"just seemed to know what to do, with neither fear nor foolish risk."* No one taught her this. Rather, these natural tendencies were from God. Her parents noticed and supported them. My parents also supported Betsy's nature-smart interests by purchasing a zoo membership so she could go often. Nature plus nurture.

Betsy remembers the name of her first pet, a fish named Zebra. In addition to other fish, she had two gerbils. Then came her beloved dog Snickers. Betsy cared so much about Snickers that she "led" her in a prayer to trust Christ as her Savior.

Nature-smart children can be quite serious about this!

Betsy began taking horseback riding lessons when she was young. I'm proud of my brother and sister-in-law for supporting Betsy's interests. For a while, Betsy's mom gave piano lessons to the daughter of Betsy's horseback riding teacher in trade. When Betsy got a new teacher and entered many 4H contests for riding Smokey Joe and for showing Snickers, her parents trusted God for the necessary funds. They sacrificed for their daughter.

I remember being in the car as we pulled up to Pleasant Hill Farm. Betsy would smell the manure, take a deep breath, and exclaim, *"I love this smell!"* The rest of us disagreed! I love how God works, though. Through Betsy's inborn nature-smart strengths, many others had their nature smart awakened or strengthened. It's never too late! Her parents, my parents, Betsy's sister and brother, and I all became more nature smart because of Betsy's interests and abilities.

Are you raising a child like Betsy? Or would you like to further awaken a child's nature smart? Keep your children's strengths, challenges, and interests in mind as you read the rest of the chapter, and you'll determine whether they have high or low nature-smart interest and high or low nature-smart ability.

NATURE SMART: OBSERVING AND UNDERSTANDING

Nature-smart children think with patterns. When they're excited, they want to go outside. They need their love and appreciation for nature respected and to be outside often. They get joy from personally participating with nature somehow. Their power is observing patterns.

Because nature-smart children use their eyes, this intelligence has close ties to picture-smartness. However, nature-smart children don't think with visuals in their mind in the same way picture-smart children do. Rather, they're very aware of their surroundings. Because they think with patterns, they notice shapes, sizes, colors, designs, and textures. Their ability allows them to remember if a bird they see is a bluebird or blue jay even if they learned this quite a while ago. They'll also know if trees they walk past are elm trees or oak trees because they remember which has leaves with rounded ends. They easily and naturally think with comparisons and contrasts. They tend to categorize easily.

According to Dr. Howard Gardner, people raised in cities and in rural settings can all be nature smart. Where they spend their developmental years will influence their interests and where and how they use their skills. Those of us raised in cities may notice lighting and reflection from downtown buildings, unique designs on doors, and patterns from peaks and rooftops. Those raised in rural settings will use this ability in nature, paying attention to differences among animals, patterns created by fields of crops, and sunsets. If they're also picture smart, they're stunned by the beauty of the night sky. If they're paying attention mostly because they're nature smart, they're thinking about how cloud patterns might affect overnight temperatures. No matter the surroundings, we all use the same skills to observe, analyze, and remember the patterns.

Weather can be an area of interest and ability for nature-smart children. They might pay attention to it, learn to accurately predict if a storm is coming, and enjoy watching the clouds. They might also easily remember which are cumulus and which are stratus. Linda, a friend who teaches special-needs children, told me about a student of hers who reads poorly and can barely add and subtract. Yet as soon as he gets to her room and gets online every morning, he gives the weather report. That is his interest and his ability.

As with other intelligences, there's a hierarchy of giftedness within nature smart. For example, I enjoy nature. In my travels, I've been privileged to see much: the snowcapped mountains of Lake Tahoe, fog rolling across the hills of Scotland, animals during safaris in Africa, and so much more. I appreciate nature; I don't need to understand it. But many children are more nature smart than I am because they want to *understand* where mountains come from, what causes fog, how elephants think.

Many years ago, I taught a one-week learning styles course at a seminary north of San Francisco. I had been told deer lived on campus. Instantly, many questions formed in my mind: How did they get here? Why do they stay? What do they eat? Why aren't they hit and killed by cars? Would they prefer to leave if they could?

When coming back from lunch one day, several deer ran across the road. I exclaimed, "What are they doing here?" This question did not spring from being nature smart. It's not one of my strengths. What smart do you think drove the question? It was my logic-smartness. I asked that question because I want things to make sense and it made no sense to me that deer lived on this busy campus.

Avoid trying to determine children's intelligence strengths based on isolated incidents and brief exposure. My question about the deer might have caused people to assume I'm nature smart. That wouldn't have been terribly serious, of course. But you can negatively affect motivation and learning if you misjudge a child's intelligence strengths and design learning activities based on that decision. So be careful. Look for consistency.

If your child asks a question like mine and it seems out of character, it may be your opportunity to awaken that smart. In other words, if you had been driving the car and your child had asked, "What are the deer doing here?" you could have taken the time to help him or her find the answer. You could have asked what other questions your child had. You could have suggested some of your own and then worked together to research the answers. This interaction might awaken your child's nature-smart part of the mind. Look and listen for these opportunities with each of the eight intelligences. Then choose to take the time to delve in and strengthen them. It will be time well spent.

What nature-smart strengths do your children have? Are they already interested in gardening? Are they able to grow vegetables well? Do they enjoy delivering extras to shut-ins and neighbors? Do they like to help you choose which colors of petunias and pansies to plant? Do they enjoy making bouquets for grandparents and friends who are sick? Do they offer to help church staff water trees and bushes? Or, do they care deeply about the environment? Do they talk with you about pollution, recycling, and collecting litter along highways? Have they formed a school committee to increase participation in recycling? Like Betsy, do your child's nature-smart strengths show up more with animals? Is your daughter impatiently waiting to be old enough to volunteer at the local animal shelter?

As with other smarts, nature-smart children will benefit from knowing that their abilities with plants, animals, and the out-of-doors spring from a part of their mind. They can be deeply encouraged to learn that they're not just *good with* animals and plants but they're *smart* because of that!

LEARNING MATTERS:
SCIENCE AND NATURE SMARTS

Some children who struggle with logic-smart sciences like chemistry and physics can be very successful at nature-smart sciences like biology, earth science, and oceanography. That's why we shouldn't allow children to believe or say they're not good at science. That's too general a statement. Your child may have struggled with logic-smart general science but aced biology.

During elementary school, science topics change frequently. Some of my second graders definitely enjoyed units on fruit flies, when they each had vials

The way children are smart influences what they respond to emotionally.

of them on their desks. They would run to their desk each morning to see what happened overnight. These were the same children who enjoyed the disks of mealworms they had on their desks a few weeks later. You can probably imagine that some children didn't like either of these units. Instead, they were enthusiastic when we studied non-nature-smart topics.

Your daughter may like science one week and not the next. Her interest and ability will have peaks and valleys. Don't assume the teacher taught badly one week or there was something wrong with the lessons. The difference can lie in which smart is necessary for the content and activities and whether your daughter knows to go to that part of her brain in order to be successful.

Smarts can do more than help children understand academics. They can also help children learn about and process emotions. Shortly after a teacher who was also a mom heard me teach about these multiple intelligences, she and her husband made the difficult decision to put down their dog. That night, they and four of their children were reminiscing when they realized their eleven-year-old son wasn't with them. She found him in his bedroom where he was making a design with his collection of seashells. His collection was important to him and finding and creating patterns calmed him. She sat with him for a while, but she discerned talking wasn't going to help this son. Maybe later he'd be ready to share.

The way children are smart influences what they respond to emotionally and how they process all emotions. Word-smart children will need to talk or write, logic-smart children will need questions answered as they try to make sense of things, picture-smart children may color and create, music-smart children will usually get lost in music they create or listen to, body-smart children may want to be physically active and may want physical contact with you, nature-smart children may categorize by patterns and may want to spend time outside, people-smart children will want to talk with others, and self-smart children will want to spend time alone with their thoughts and feelings. Since this eleven-year-old boy was alone in his room, my guess is that he isn't just nature smart but that he is self-smart, too. All the stories and feelings his siblings and parents were discussing would have overwhelmed him.

All of this is true for adults, of course, too. Many who hear me speak admit they wish they were better understood by their spouse. They tell me they're not allowed to process feelings or even feel but are often told to "just get over it." That's dismissive. They describe their hearts as being heavy. If this is relevant to you and relationships with family and coworkers, perhaps these thoughts will empower you to have a necessary conversation.

Strengthening Nature Smart: Teachable Moments

You can strengthen children's nature smart by helping them see details in their environments and in animals and plants. Point them out and talk about them using specific language that draws attention to design elements, similarities, and differences. You can also use games and activities that help them see patterns. This can be as simple as showing your son several designs and having him identify the two that match.

Teach your child how to compare, contrast, and categorize.[1] Encourage them to collect things and talk with them about their collections. You can also create opportunities for your child to interact with animals and to investigate things outside. These experiences will be most successful when you have clear and specific purposes.

Also, be alert to teachable moments. With all the smarts, these can be the best ways to awaken and strengthen children's intelligences. For example, perhaps your young son saw a worm on the driveway after a rainstorm. He stared at it, touched it, and wanted to know all about it. Perhaps you were concerned about his short attention span until he discovered this worm. Now he is so focused you have a hard time getting him to think about anything else. God used this worm to awaken your son's nature smart. If you spend time with your son exploring worms, go to websites for information, and read library books about worms, you strengthen his nature smart further. Think about it this way: The worm on your driveway cracked the nature-smart door open. When you answered your son's questions and got interested with him, the door opened farther. If you link his interest in worms to other animals, the door will stay open. Work with God. He gave your son the worm. You get to do something with it. This is your privilege!

Learning Struggles

I'm concerned that nature smart is being awakened later in many children because of technology. They are inside playing games and spending time on social media. They're missing out on the joys of playing outside, getting dirty as they explore things, and having their nature smart awakened. You might not think this is serious because it's "just nature." But what if these children were designed by God to be the next great nature scientists? Remember, the nurture you provides matters. Plus, the ability to distinguish patterns is helpful. And the out-of-doors can be so much fun!

I know of a child who defiantly declared he didn't need to go to the mountains on vacation with his family because he had seen them. His father didn't understand because he knew his son had never been to the mountains. After a minute, the son pointed to a picture of mountains on his device and yelled, "See!!" The dad cringed as he responded, "Those aren't mountains! That's a picture of mountains!"

Nature-smart children's attitudes can become negative if they're inside for long stretches, especially if there aren't windows. They can become restless. Under these circumstances, they may become more irritable and critical toward other children. These attitudes can then negatively influence learning.

Unless there are pets at home, being inside all the time can paralyze this intelligence, if it had been awakened already. Other things that paralyze nature smart include never being allowed to play outside, not having collections honored, and never creating opportunities for your child who wants a dog or cat to spend time with one.

Teaching the Nature-Smart Child: Find the Patterns!

Nature-smart children benefit when we help them relate what they're studying to nature. This can increase their attention, enhance their motivation, and help them remember the information. For example, within history, they may be fascinated by how explorers used the stars for navigation, tracked animals for food, and made canoes with handmade tools. In science, they could study how animals are camouflaged in their environments. If your nature-smart son needs Scripture to study, he may be motivated by Psalm 23 and the parable of the sower found in Matthew 13.

Because these children naturally look for patterns and notice similarities and differences, they'll enjoy using microscopes, binoculars, and magnifying glasses. They may collect and categorize things by shape, color, design, texture, and such. This may be why they remember details about the variety of fauna and flora in their state. (Do you consider yourself word smart, but you're unfamiliar with the words *fauna* [animals] and *flora* [plants]? Perhaps this is because you're not terribly nature smart. Remember—our intelligences don't work alone.)

Attending to patterns can help when your child studies things such as poetry, multiplication, prefixes on vocabulary words, and design elements in art class. Learning cursive letters, distinguishing among triangles in a geometry assignment, and remembering formulas in physics can all be made easier when your child discovers patterns.[2]

Studying outside can also benefit these children. During my programs, I often ask how many children would like to be outside. About half the children raise their hands. They tell me that being surrounded by nature seems to add to their joy. Note, however, that some nature-smart children might find being outside too distracting to study just as some music-smart children can't listen to music when studying and some can. Children who want to study outside might need to prove they can finish their assignments efficiently and effectively in that setting. Some might look for insects in the grass, watch the clouds, and think about running and playing, riding their bikes, kicking rocks, and the last time they camped out.

WHEN THEY GROW UP: CAREERS AND EDUCATION

Each science discipline with links to nature has careers associated with it. Every animal shelter needs employees. So do florist shops, camps, and recycling centers. Your children might also want to consider careers like these: tree surgeon, forest or park ranger, veterinarian or veterinarian's assistant, environmental inspector, landscape designer, nature photographer, missionary, field biologist, and pet sitter.

RELATIONSHIPS

Enjoying God's World Together

When two or more nature-smart children form a friendship, you can almost always count on them being outside more than inside. They'll spend time going to parks, zoos, and the pool. They'll also enjoy getting dirty together from exploring something they discovered. Children who tell me they have nature-smart strengths tell me they like to get dirty. They like it!

Since I was raised in a large city, my nature-smart patterning interest shows up mostly in cities. This has been especially evident when I travel overseas where architecture is stunning. I thoroughly enjoy it.

I recently traveled to Hungary, to speak to missionaries about the educational needs of their children. After the conference, a group of us toured sites in Budapest. I've been there many times, but enjoyed experiencing this beautiful city through the eyes of others who have not been there.

Suzanne, Ansley, and Monica behaved like I did the first few times I was there. They took pictures of buildings. They noticed the shapes, shadows, lights, heights, designs, and colors. The constant, "Look at that!" made it such a fun few days. Our nature-smart patterning ability caused us all to enjoy architecture. It bonded us and it's something we can talk about when we see each other.

Budapest was enjoyable and rich because I was with people similar to me. But being with people *not* like me has also made experiences more enjoyable. Going on a safari, visiting zoos, and spending time at botanical gardens with friends who both enjoy *and* know a lot about plants and animals always make these adventures better.

There are keys to us having fun together. My friends have to respect that I may not be as interested in details as they are. And I have to be humble and not embarrassed that I don't know what they know. It has to be okay with me *and* them that I sometimes don't care that I don't know. Believe me, this hasn't always been the case with me. (Ask my friends!) Understanding there are eight different smarts and it's okay to not have all eight as strengths has freed even me to be more comfortable with who I am.

Relating to Parents: Match Chores to Smarts?

When needing to have important conversations with nature-smart children, I recommend you remember their love of the outdoors. If possible, talk with them outside, in the backyard, or while you're walking in the neighborhood together. This is wise for couples to remember, too. Even choosing a restaurant table by a window can lead to more productive conversations than you'd have in the middle of the room. (When arriving at restaurants with one particular friend, she always asks for a booth by a window. Always!)

What did you learn about nature-smart children being able to place appropriate security in their parents in the story of my niece Betsy from the beginning of this chapter? She learned she could trust her parents when they responded well to her obvious love of animals and arranged for her horseback riding lessons. I doubt that Betsy is any different from your children. They notice when you listen to them, appreciate what intrigues them, answer their questions, and explore outside with them.

In the chapter about body-smart children, I wrote that chores can be used to awaken and strengthen the smart. Knowing your child and matching chores to how he or she is smart can be a powerful way to honor each of them. There are certain things all children must do regardless of how they are smart. This is true for adults, too! It's not okay to say, "I'm not very smart in the way that would make this easy so I'm not doing it." Oh no! But, imagine if we did match chores to smarts when possible. Might we get greater cooperation? More excellence?

When we know and respect how our children are wired, it affirms the freedom they have to be themselves.

Jill Savage, my coauthor of *No More Perfect Kids*, wrote about this in regard to her son Austin:

There are always times we may require our kids to do something they don't like. My kids have never "liked" working in the yard, but we live on two-and-a-half acres so, whether they like it or not, they mow the lawn and help outside on a regular basis. Some of that is about learning responsibility and stewardship. It's about building character. However, when I go out to weed one of our flower gardens, I resist the urge to invite my son to join me. I enjoy the sense of accomplishment weeding gives me, but he does not. No amount of wishing he loved it will change that. I need to know that about him and respect that in him.

However, if I need my son to help me weed because we're getting ready to host a picnic, I will ask, "Austin, I need your help weeding this afternoon. I know it's one of your least favorite things to do, but I also know you enjoy having your friends over to hang out in the yard. We need to work together to get this done so we can all enjoy the yard we have." When we know and respect how our kids are wired, it affirms the freedom they have to be themselves.[3]

SPIRITUAL GROWTH

Connecting with the Creator

Children who are very nature smart will more likely connect with God as Creator than others might. They may have more questions about natural disasters than children who aren't as nature smart. Earthquakes, tornadoes, hurricanes, and wildfires may cause anxiety, concern, and curiosity. You can discuss passages such as Psalm 46 and Psalm 107. Respecting their questions and statements will help them grow in their ability to trust God.

As you've learned in other chapters, how we are smart can also influence how we prefer to worship. I know a number of adults with definite nature-smart strengths who easily worship God while sitting on a bench overlooking a wooded area and while sitting on the sand listening to ocean waves. In these environments, they immediately think of God's creativity.

When did these preferences begin? When their nature smart was awakened. People whose nature smart was activated in childhood describe rich times with God while at church camps and while walking in the woods with their families. If it was awakened later, they've enjoyed the more recent discovery of how valuable being outside can be to their spiritual growth. If you believe your children have nature-smart strengths, encourage them to connect with God outside and through His wonderful creations.

Scripture that God might especially use to draw these children to Himself and to mature them into Christlikeness include the creation story from Genesis 1, the story of Noah (Genesis 6–9), and miracles like the parting of the Red Sea (Exodus 14). Analogies such as the sheep and shepherd (e.g., John 10) and eagle and eaglet (e.g., Deuteronomy 32:11; Psalm 103:1–5), can also be very effective. Parables such as the parable of the weeds (Matthew 13:24–30, 36–43) will often easily communicate truth to those who are interested in nature. So will the many Psalms that include nature.

CHARACTER:
BE SMART WITH YOUR NATURE SMART

Caring for All God's Creatures

Some children with nature-smart strengths might be tempted to worship the created instead of the Creator. As friends of mine concluded, they might confuse the "awe" of nature for God.

Have you heard about dogs trained to fight? I wonder if people who train them are nature smart, but then they cross the line.

Somehow the thrill of the battle, potential for victory, and money that may be involved influence them to take a definite talent and twist it for harm. It's sad.

Most children who have pets when they're young will continue to value animals. Not only that, but the character they developed while taking care of their pets will continue to serve them well. There may be no better way to develop responsibility than to share a pet. When an only child or siblings have to feed pets and clean and walk some, they can learn time management, cooperation, diligence, and other qualities.

Let's Play!

Play *Qwirkle*: Match colors and shapes and use wise maneuvers and a strategy to win.

Play *Rock On Geology Game*: Rock and mineral collection includes fifteen specimens and fifty-plus polished rocks and minerals; five levels of play.

I AM PEOPLE SMART: I THINK WITH PEOPLE

W hen walking up to your parents to ask them a favor, how many of you can figure out whether they might say no by just looking at them?"

Lots of children raise their hands.

"How many of you then don't even ask your question but turn around instead?"

Laughter erupts.

"Your dad asks, 'Can I help you?'"

"You respond 'No!' as you keep walking away because you want him to say 'Yes' and he has 'No' written all over his body."

More laughter as they wave their hands at me to make sure I notice they do this.

"If you can do this, it's because you're people smart. Good for you!"

I enjoy this part of my program for children. I get to explain they're smart if they can read body language well and respond appropriately. I love encouraging them!

Hearing hundreds of children proclaim "I am people smart! I will be smart with my smarts!" never gets old.

Based on numerous conversations with children, I'm certain at least some of the people-smart children in the audience haven't felt smart. They may not have strengths in the smarts closely tied to core academic classes of science, math, history, and reading. Or it's possible their people-smart strengths have gotten them into trouble so they don't value the skills they have.

These children can comfort others after determining they're sad.

Of course, there's much more to being people smart. Let's find out which of your children have these abilities and which ones could afford to have them strengthened.

PEOPLE SMART: THINKING BY CONNECTING

People-smart children think with people. When they're excited, they talk more to more people. They need people to listen to them, interact with them, and react to their ideas. They get joy from sharing what they know and from understanding people. Thinking by connecting is their power.

As demonstrated in my slice of a student program, being

people smart includes the definite strength of reading body language. These children know if someone is mad, glad, or sad. If your child is able to discern that you're concerned and not angry, or content and not bored, it's because he or she is people smart.

At the high end of the people-smart hierarchy is the child who can accurately discern someone's mood, intention, and desire *as well as* respond appropriately. For example, as some people-smart children talk, they can discern listeners' reactions by observing changing facial expressions and body language. Have you noticed your son doing this? When he comes to you with a question, do you ever think he's going in one direction, only to have him change his question midstream? Maybe he observed something in your reactions that concerned him. He didn't want you to answer "no," so he changed the wording of his question in hopes of getting a "maybe" or "yes" response.

These children can comfort others after determining they're sad and give you some space when they discern you're disappointed. They know to befriend the lonely and why a small group isn't working well. They can recognize someone's joy and choose to ask about it so they can share in the experience. I highly value friends of mine who choose to do this. In return, I look for opportunities to put them first and respond to the feelings I sense in them. This give-and-take strengthens our friendships. Married friends tell me being people smart in these ways definitely helps their marriage.

The opposite are children who walk right up to you and are clueless about your mood. They may begin to tell you about their day, not noticing you're deep in thought. They may not notice you're concentrating on a task and get quickly upset when you don't immediately break away to pay attention to them.

The abilities of children to read and respond well to facial expressions, body language, and tone of voice are among the important reasons to awaken this smart early. It's what helps children choose friends and form healthy friendships. It allows them to discern who is for them and who is against them. It's how they know who to give a second chance to and who to stay away from for at least a while after they've been hurt.

Yet because of texting, handheld devices, and eyes looking down, this smart is being awakened later than in the past. I've seen far too many parents answer children's questions without ever looking up from their game or social media feed. And, of course, I've seen children do the same.

People smart is rich, like other smarts, with multiple facets. It doesn't just explain friendships. It also explains why some people think well with others. The ability to interpret facial reactions, body language, and tone of voice stimulates thinking. It's one of my strengths and, initially, new friends and staff can find it confusing. I might talk to them, not need them to say anything, but say "Thank you" as I leave the room. They come to understand that I observed reactions that didn't need to be accompanied by words. Did they react with surprise at my idea? Did they quickly look confused or amused? I use their reactions to know how to keep thinking about ideas.

Those of us who are people smart especially like bouncing ideas back and forth. It's a strength. We think well with others and it's a huge part of our belonging. We sometimes don't know if our ideas are good until we hear ourselves verbalize them and watch and hear someone respond. Just as others help us refine our ideas, we can help them refine theirs. Children enjoy finding out this is normal for many of us and evidence of a specific smart.

People-smart children, who need people to think with, are different from extroverts who make friends easily and are energized by people.[1] Children and adults can be both people smart and extroverted. If so, they will especially be known for being surrounded by others because they need them for energy *and* for thinking.

Because of texting, handheld devices, and eyes looking down, this smart is being awakened later than the past.

If your daughter is extroverted, but not people smart, she'll want to *be* with people, but won't necessarily need to *think* with them. It's more about their presence and the energy they collectively create. Remember to use the interactive online checklist to help you determine whether she is people smart.

While people-smart extroverts have internal consistency, if

your son is people smart and an introvert, he may be confused and he may confuse others. Introverts tend to keep their ideas to themselves and get their energy when they're alone.[2] They often avoid people because they drain them. Can you feel the conflict? He needs to be with people to get his thoughts clarified, but he doesn't want to be with people because fatigue will set in. He's stuck. He can be unsure of himself. To his friends, he can appear inconsistent and they can get frustrated. Your son will benefit from feedback you provide as you observe him in different settings. As you decrease his frustration by helping him navigate different situations, you'll increase his security and clarify his identity.

The extroverted/people-smart design and introverted/people-smart design can be as confusing and important to understand for adults as they are for children. If you think one or the other might explain some of your internal confusion and relationship struggles, read these four paragraphs again. Or maybe this might be relevant for your spouse, parents, or coworkers. I've found too many people have been forced into limiting boxes. "Oh, you're extroverted. Therefore, you _____." But, it's not that simple. We're not that simple. God creates us to be successful so we often have dynamic facets that internally may conflict and confuse us. But, if we don't allow them to be paralyzed but choose to understand them instead, we can be freed to be who God intended for us to be when He chose in His love to make us, us. Yes!

LEARNING MATTERS:
PEOPLE SMARTS AND SCHOOL SUCCESS

We were created to make a positive difference in the world. To leave the world a better place. To solve problems. To love well. Because it's virtually impossible to do any of this consistently well without people-smart abilities, this intelligence is valuable to learning. It makes life more vivid and positive. It matters to school and life, for today and tomorrow.

Because all of school requires interacting with peers and adult authority figures, knowing how to read people well decreases stress and increases relational success. Paying attention and cooperating is easier. People-smart children will know how *not* to irritate others, get on their bad side, distract them, and more. Relational obedience all comes more naturally. Focus is affected. Learning increases.

When your daughter is young, teachers may tell you, "Your daughter plays well with others." When she's older, you may hear, "Your daughter is a cooperative member of small groups." About your son, you may hear, "He's always aware of how to be helpful and I appreciate his servant's heart." Also, "Your son is able to be persuasive without being bossy and rude. He just has a great way with his peers."

Strengthening People Smart: Being Present with Others

Putting handheld devices away and using technology less is almost guaranteed to increase children's sensitivity to others. When we choose to engage in conversations and make eye contact, children will find out that being fully present with people can be enjoyable and helpful. Now we can talk about reading eye contact, facial expressions, and body language.

You can also help children learn to read body language clues and respond appropriately by teaching them how you interpret what you do. If you determined that someone waiting in line ahead of you at the store was worried and not just frustrated, tell your child later how you discerned that. Was it what you heard and/or things you saw? Teach them how you can tell the differences between satisfaction, joy, and eagerness, and between laziness, confusion, and fear. Explain how you decide when to speak up and when to remain silent.

Watching television shows and movies together in order to discuss what you observe in the characters can be effective. I have friends who watch some shows with the volume turned off. Helping their children predict if characters are mad, telling the truth, manipulating others, or in love just based on body language, facial reactions, and interactions can be very instructive. Analyzing dialogue in literature can be equally beneficial.

Children without people-smart strengths can also have this

intelligence stretched and improved when they're placed in safe small groups. Choose wisely, though. Expecting them to work with loud, confident brainstormers and quick thinkers might backfire and actually paralyze any people-smart confidence and abilities they were beginning to cultivate. First, they need to gain confidence in sharing and having their ideas critiqued.

Learning Struggles: When to Talk—and When Not To

People-smart children benefit when teachers, coaches, pastors, and parents understand they talk when they get excited. They often talk to peers, even when they shouldn't (such as in the middle of class). They may initiate the conversations or eagerly respond if another student talks to them. Often their talking is a spontaneous response to their joy of discovery. Their interactions express high energy; connection is the source of their power. They obviously need to use self-control and learn to discern when talking up is appropriate.

The greatest challenge for most people-smart children is to be without input for any lengthy period. They can most likely handle being alone for a while, but because they think best with others and are most confident of their own ideas when they share with others, they'll struggle if they're alone too much. They also might reach out to you more often than their siblings might.

Teaching the People-Smart Child: Brainstorming!

Role-plays, dramas, demonstrations, discussions, and connecting with mentors works well for people-smart children.[3] They also may enjoy reading biographies and autobiographies of men and women they would find interesting. And that will depend upon other smarts. For instance, they may enjoy reading about scientists, athletes, musicians, or authors.

It's especially effective to allow these children to work with partners and complete projects with small groups. In those settings, they can ask questions, answer questions, and get reactions to their ideas. This also might be why they'll do their homework better with you nearby than down the hall in their quiet bedroom.

Another idea is to have these children brainstorm with peers (or you) for a few minutes as they begin working on their assignment. Then they can return to their seats to work alone. For example, if they're told to begin a creative writing assignment, children with people-smart strengths may struggle with writer's block. They may not know what they know. They will lack confidence in their ideas. Allowing these children a few minutes to talk with others about their preliminary ideas can help them get started.

Remind your people-smart daughter to use her ability to pick up important clues while listening to you and teachers. For instance, she can determine what content her teacher will stress on the test as his voice, gestures, and body language change during the review. She'll know what to study in more depth and her grade may reflect it.

WHEN THEY GROW UP:
CAREERS AND EDUCATION

My trainer is people smart and I'm glad. By looking into my eyes and at my face, she can tell whether to change the weight she has me using or the number of repetitions I complete. Her use of this ability increases my security in her. My niece Betsy uses her ability when looking at people who come to the emergency room. She can discern if what they're saying lines up with how they look. She can sometimes choose tests to run based on their eyes and facial reactions to her questions.

Administrators, pastors, and others in positions of leadership benefit from being people smart. Their skills allow them to relate well and connect to people they work with and serve. They understand what people need and can determine how to meet their needs.

Other careers that fit the people-smart profile well include counselors, politicians, lawyers, social workers, evangelists, receptionists, travel agents, advertisers, personnel directors, talk-show hosts, doctors, nurses, consultants, salespeople, police officers, reporters, missionaries, inventors, and waiters and waitresses. Much of their effectiveness will depend on both reading body language and listening to what people say.

RELATIONSHIPS:
LEARNING TO LEAD

People-smart children tend to make friends easily, partly because they understand people. More than others, they'll probably be able to identify who might like them, who they will like, and who will be good for them in one way or another. They people-watch at the mall, at the basketball game, and maybe during math class. Of course, this isn't a wise use of brain power if it means they're not listening to their teacher.

People-smart children can build consensus and increase peace.

In order to spend time with others, people-smart children may join athletic teams, academic teams such as debate and forensics, work teams such as yearbook and student council, and music groups such as choir and band. They may also be the popular ones who others want to eat lunch with and sit with during sporting events.

Other children may want to be friends with your people-smart daughter because of her natural leadership gifts and willingness and ability to express compassion. This can result in her having relationships with hurting and troubled children in need of a confident leader. This will be especially true if your daughter also has logic-smart strengths. As it did initially with me and Tina, this combination elevates her problem-solving abilities and makes her even more attractive to peers with problems they want solved.

Unfortunately, the same ability people-smart children use to choose friends can also be used for unhealthy purposes. For example, if your people-smart son decides he wants to begin cheating, he might know who to ask for help. Because he's an excellent observer of people, he probably knows who has been getting away with it. After choosing who to ask, he'll most likely be able to ask for help in such a way that the other child will say yes. Gang leaders come to mind as a powerful example of this misguided ability. They know who to target for joining their gang, and they know who to target for attack. That's why they become leaders. What a sad example of using a strength in the wrong way!

Another potential relationship challenge can arise when children and adults have something to hide. For example, I've talked with children who are being abused. Because they don't want anyone to know, they've told me about avoiding children and adults who "seem to figure things out on their own." These are probably people with people-smart strengths.

People-smart children can build consensus and increase peace. They can successfully rally their peers to care about things from class assignments to a special worship concert taking place on Friday night. Better than others, they might be able to plan parties and make decisions about what activities, food, and music would be popular.

Evangelism among their peers and family members might

come naturally to people-smart children because they can discern who is ready to hear the gospel. They may instinctively know how to turn a conversation to spiritual things, which evangelism approach to use, and which verses and personal illustrations to share. They also may efficiently and effectively disciple others to grow in their faith. They may be able to predict what questions people have, what topics to bring up next, which spiritual disciplines will be best, and the like.

In a similar way, people-smart children may be drawn to service because they can often discern people's needs. They may know if one of their friends is frustrated, depressed, or angry and what they can do to help. Without directly asking, they may know if a family from the church would prefer meals brought in, groceries so they can cook their own food, or restaurant gift cards. Because they know many people, they'll know who might help them with their projects. Then they can use their team-building skills to increase the group's cohesiveness, efficiency, and effectiveness.

As I've cautioned you before, make sure to look for a broad pattern of abilities when deciding if your child has strengths in any of these intelligences. Even if the above paragraph doesn't exactly describe your child, he or she may be very people smart. How is that possible? There are at least two reasons.

First, as I explained earlier, children can be people smart and introverted. This personality dimension causes children to gravitate toward their inner world. They are quiet, reflective thinkers. They are fatigued by being with people and energized by being alone.[4] There will be times when their introverted personality type will camouflage their people-smart strengths.

Second, it's possible to have both people-smart and self-smart strengths. As I'll explain more fully in the next chapter, self-smart children think deeply inside of themselves and need quiet and privacy. They don't need people to think with. Therefore, children with strengths in both of these intelligences probably won't have as many friends as children who are much more people smart than they are self-smart. Also, if they're both people smart and self-smart, and their self-smart is most activated for a particular reason, it may appear that these children no longer have people-smart strengths. That's not the case.

A pattern I'm aware of is children who behave in very people-smart ways at school, but in self-smart ways at home, where they crave quiet, peace, space, and privacy. They tell me they used up all their people-smart energy at school. Is it any wonder that sometimes, during parent-teacher conferences, parents think teachers are talking about someone else's child?

Relating to Parents: Talk *with*, Not At

One of the most important things to remember about people-smart children is that they think best when bouncing ideas back and forth. So to increase their trust in you, talk *with* them rather than *at* them. During these conversations, you can model excellent cause-effect thinking and commonsense reasoning. Ask questions, answer theirs, react to ideas, etc. If they arrive at their own wise conclusions, they'll more likely follow them than if you would have told them the very same thing.

When someone in the family suggests an idea, it's honoring to ask people-smart children, "What do you think?" Of course, your children will need the maturity to understand that what they think won't always influence your thinking. In addition, because they're very plugged in to how others think, it might pay to ask the question, "What would your friends think?"

People-smart children will not trust parents who are hypocrites. I'm not sure other children will either! It's just that children who are people smart are more likely to know when their parents are being hypocritical. You need to remember that your body language is as important as your words. If you say "I love you," but your body language and lack of eye contact indicate disinterest, your child may question your love.

SPIRITUAL GROWTH

His Love, His Mercy, His People

God is extremely people smart. That's an understatement, isn't it? When people-smart children recognize what they have in common with their Creator, their trust in Him will increase. For example, we see that Jesus related differently to the lost, the Pharisees, and His disciples. He knew what would be best for each type of person. People-smart children are able to do the same thing.

Some people-smart children may connect better to Jesus Christ than to God because Jesus seems more identifiable to them. They'll also benefit from learning about God's attributes that relate to interacting with people. Love, mercy, grace, forgiveness, truth . . .

Because people-smart children think best with others, they may grow in their faith most when with others. They'll gravitate to group activities where they're allowed to talk and share their ideas. Their other intelligences, personality, and experiences can influence what types of groups fit them best. They may connect well with God at summer camp, youth group, Sunday school, and/or during one-on-one mentoring times. They may struggle to worship alone and to learn alone.

They will get more from worship services and children's church if they know they'll get to share their insights with you after the services. For instance, I know an older teen who listens better to her pastor's sermons ever since her parents told her they'd react to her conclusions and answer her questions on Sunday afternoons. These discussions have provided rich bonding times.

Family devotions may be more important to them than their own quiet time. This, of course, won't be the case if you don't

There is a very fine line between our strengths and our sins.

allow them to talk. That would frustrate them terribly. Remember, they need to interact with ideas.

There might be nothing more important than children's spiritual growth so considering the eight great smarts when planning for it can be life-giving. But, just as with so much else I've written about, it's true for adults, too. A woman shared this with me about her husband: "I used to think about my husband, 'Why don't you just sit down and read your Bible, for crying out loud!' Well, guess what? His strength is not word smart! He loves the audio Bible, worship music, prayer, and being in groups with others to grow his faith. I have gained some understanding! I have more grace for my husband."

CHARACTER:
BE SMART WITH YOUR PEOPLE SMART

Persuading or Manipulating?

During my student programs on this topic, I usually ask this question: "How many of you have asked your parents a question and gotten them to say 'yes' when you know they should have said 'no'?"

Can you guess the percentage of students who raise their hands? I'd say at least 75 percent! They laugh, and it appears they feel quite proud of themselves. I admit I can do it, too, but that I don't want to. Their mood changes when I say, "Let's not ever be proud of this! Let's use our talents only for good!"

There is a very fine line between our strengths and our sins. People-smart children are great motivators. They can also be great manipulators. Watch them with brothers and sisters! Different character qualities and views of people determine how they use their skills.

Just as word-smart children need self-control so they don't talk all the time, so do people-smart children. In fact, if like me, your children have word-smart and people-smart strengths, they probably want to talk all the time! This doesn't mean they should be allowed to. On the contrary, they must learn self-discipline, self-respect, and respect for others. Without these character qualities, paralysis might set in as they're told to be quiet and stop bothering their classmates, siblings, and you.

I wonder if this other issue is relevant to you. Because people-smart children like people, they might talk to just about anyone. Recently, a mom contacted me about this very issue. While parked in a lot, her daughter looked out the car window and talked with a couple. They were on motorcycles, dressed in full biker leather, and covered in tattoos. Her daughter had very little, if any, experience with people like this, but she immediately asked about their bikes, if they had grandkids, and how long they have been married. Afterward, this mom talked with her daughter *again* about "stranger danger." Her daughter looked up, smiled, and declared, "But they looked kind and I could tell the lady was a grandma."

Talk often with people-smart children about boundaries. Usually their abilities to read people can be trusted, but they're not immune to being manipulated. Model and explain how you decide when to talk and when you know it's not necessary or appropriate. Let your child know you're glad he or she easily expresses love and interest, but that silence is sometimes best. Watch to make sure paralysis doesn't set in.

Let's Play!

Play *Headbanz*: Everyone but you knows what role you've been assigned. Ask questions to try to figure it out before you run out of time. You could be a mouse, dirty sock, or cash register.

Play *Guesstures*: You only have a few seconds to use classic charades techniques to get your team to guess the word on your assigned card.

I AM SELF-SMART:
I THINK WITH REFLECTION

If you've ever asked children to make a simple choice that ended up being anything but simple, it's possible they were self-smart. These children like choice. But because they relate learning to their lives, think deeply, and want everything to feel right, choosing can be challenging.

For example, you might ask your son or daughter to choose a piece of colored paper for an activity, assuming it will just take a minute. But inside his or her head, this occurs:

I could choose yellow, but I'm not happy enough to choose yellow. Orange is a pumpkin color and it's not even fall. I can't choose blue because Evan chose blue and I don't like him today. I used green last time so I can't choose green again. That wouldn't be good. Daddy said sometimes red is an angry color or something and I'm not angry. Purple is a nice color. Purple. Yes, I like purple. I wish it was lavender. I just learned that word and color and I like it. I wish Mom had lavender. I guess I'll choose purple.

Sound familiar? All of that went on inside your child's head, which is what self-smart children do. They think deeply and personally. Halfway through, if you were tempted to shout, *"Choose a piece of paper!!"* you're not alone. Some self-smart children and adults tell me they even frustrate themselves because nothing's ever simple!

There's more to being self-smart. Ready to find out? Great!

SELF-SMART:
TO REFLECT AND KNOW

Self-smart children think with reflection deeply inside of themselves and relate learning to their lives. When they're excited, they want to spend time by themselves thinking more. They need quiet, peace, privacy, and space. They get joy from knowing what they know. Their power is reflection and the knowing that comes from it.

When studying and learning, self-smart children want to understand things in depth. This takes time. Answering questions takes time, too. They want to consider all their knowledge before answering and they want to get answers right. Therefore, they can frustrate teachers and peers and think of themselves as slow thinkers. This is a reason they often don't feel smart.

More than other children, they may want to "sleep on their ideas." If you force them to quickly share or if anyone belittles their "slowness," paralysis may set in. They may stop reflecting altogether.

Because self-smart children know what they believe and why, they're usually able to stand up for their beliefs. They may become active in a cause, perhaps in a behind-the-scenes role, or they may just talk with friends and peers when the issue comes up in conversation. Their willingness to promote their convictions and opinions will depend, in part, on whether they are also people smart or logic smart. Remember, these intelligences don't work alone. With people-smart strengths and/or logic-smart strengths, it's more likely that self-smart children can persuade others.

Self-smart children know their strengths and weaknesses.

Self-smart children tend to be quiet, independent workers and thinkers. When they're excited, they enjoy going off by themselves to reflect on their feelings and thoughts. They don't need others to help them know what they know. They don't need to tell others what they know. In these ways, self-smart children and people-smart children are opposites.

Self-smart children may describe themselves as loners, thinkers, quiet, aware, and careful. As I've cautioned you before, make sure you look for broad patterns that indicate children have this intelligence strength before you assume they do. For example, children who are introverted by personality may say they're loners. Children who have been neglected, abused, or hurt emotionally may behave like loners. This doesn't necessarily mean, however, that they're self-smart. Evidence of self-smart strengths include that they think deeply and privately and enjoy relating learning to their lives.

Self-smart children know themselves well. They know their strengths and weaknesses. They know what ticks them off, turns them on, and calms them down. They know what interests them, what they like, what they want, and what they need. They're able to use this self-understanding to guide and enrich their lives.

Similar internal confusion can occur for self-smart children who are extroverted that occurs for people-smart children who are introverted. I addressed that in the last chapter. Self-smart children need to be alone with their thoughts. Extroverted children need to be with people for their energy.[1] Therefore, there will be times when these children are conflicted . . . should I be with my peers and family now or not? They can confuse themselves and others and send mixed messages that make it hard to know for sure how to relate to them. On the other hand, self-smart children who are introverted[2] by personality will have even more need to spend time alone.

Another issue consistently comes up when I speak on these intelligences. Parents and teachers ask if I think children on the Autism Spectrum Disorder may be self-smart. It's certainly true that they appear to have similar strengths and needs. After a mom heard me speak, she sent me this message:

Another daughter of mine has always been very shy, and has been diagnosed with Asperger's. Social situations can be very difficult for her. But I have learned that she is very self-smart, and have encouraged her to know that she can set boundaries around social occasions. She knows that if we have a *family* event coming up, she needs to have quiet ahead of time and after. About six hours is her limit on being able to handle those situations. And she will quietly let me know if she is "done" before that. I feel like before [knowing about the smarts] I might have pushed her, but now I encourage her. She is also picture smart and uses drawing as a way to calm herself.

LEARNING MATTERS: BUILDING CONFIDENCE

The sheer number of people at school can make school overwhelming for children with self-smart strengths. They don't want or need lots of input and prefer to think alone with the information they have. People can distract them. These are reasons homeschooling can work well for self-smart children.

Self-smart children often have excellent insights because of their deep-and-wide thinking. If they can realize how much others may benefit from their conclusions, and develop the courage to share, their confidence can increase. When others appreciate their ideas and benefit from them, these self-smart children may develop connections and motivation to move beyond their comfort zone more often. This, in turn, can all serve to awaken and strengthen their people smart.

Strengthening Self-Smart: Learning and Life

To increase children's self-smart, you can honor their need for privacy, but still ask for their input during lessons. To help children go deep and wrestle with their own thoughts, you can provide questions that direct their thinking. You can help them form and word their opinions, learn to defend them, but also learn to be open to other people's ideas. Also watch to see when they feel good about what they know and help them recognize and feel encouraged by that joy.

Self-smart children relate learning to their lives. Therefore, to be successful, they need to know who they are. Help them gain personal understanding. Privately talk about what you notice and encourage them to own things that are true about them.

Learning Struggles: Playing the Game of School

School can be uncomfortable for these children because they're regularly required to share their ideas with others. They're called on during discussions, they may be assigned to small groups, and they need to respond when you ask questions about what they're studying. All of this stresses self-smart children. Because these children prefer to study alone, your desire to interact with them can create conflict. Everybody's "interference" (a word some self-smart children use when I talk with them) can make school and learning very stressful.

These children need to be willing to play the game of school—to answer teachers' questions even if doing so doesn't enhance their own understanding. Although highly self-smart children are satisfied knowing what they know, and it's not important to them that others know, you can encourage them to participate in class and completely answer their teachers' questions. If they don't, their grades may not always reflect their true knowledge or abilities. It goes beyond that, however.

Since self-smart children are quiet and find it difficult to talk with their teachers, their teachers may not know them well. Nevertheless, it's crucial that they do! I've found that teachers may judge self-smart children harshly just because they don't understand them. They may think they're disinterested, too quiet, standoffish, and prideful. This is where you can step in as your child's advocate. You may need to help teachers understand your child's self-smart strengths and the difficulties they sometimes cause.

Teaching Your Self-Smart Child: "What Does This Have to Do with Me?"

Self-smart children benefit from individualized instruction and assignments they can complete independently. Class discussions can be very stressful. It takes longer for self-smart children to choose an answer and being vulnerable with their peers isn't easy. Therefore, they can try to predict questions teachers may use in discussions as they read assignments, watch videos, and listen to lectures. Then, when hearing a question they're willing to answer, they'd be wise to volunteer. Never participating isn't wise.[3]

Children will benefit from connecting topics to their personal lives. They like relating learning to their lives. You can look over their homework and help them determine how the topics are relevant and how they might be relevant in the future. More than other children, they may balk at participating in activities they believe have no personal benefit. In school and in life, they may ask, "What does this have to do with me?"

These children need you to help them find friends rather than just telling them to find friends.

Self-smart children like choices and options. These can be simple—write in cursive or print, do the first or second set of ten problems, and read a biography or mystery for their next book report. Of course, being given a choice is a privilege. If they complain about their options or take too long to decide, tell them they've lost the privilege. Then tell them specifically what to do.

WHEN THEY GROW UP:
CAREERS AND EDUCATION

Self-smart children may prefer careers they can do alone. However, depending on other intelligence strengths, they may want to relate to people during at least part of their day or week. For instance, they may be interested in sales or research because they can be on their own sometimes, but they can also interact with others as they need to.

Being self-employed and doing something they have great passion for may be an excellent fit. They'll need to have enough people-smart skills to understand how to sell their product or motivate people to be interested in their ideas. Self-smart children may turn out to be successful entrepreneurs. They may start a company, turn it over to others, and go start another company. They might become private investigators or writers.

Because they're in touch with their own thoughts and feelings, they may be able to help others get in touch with theirs. Like people-smart children, they may become excellent pastors, counselors, social workers, teachers, and therapists. They'll need to be confident and secure in order to be successful. Because they enjoy thinking about the future, they may want to consider becoming guidance counselors. A personal trainer may also be a good fit.

RELATIONSHIPS:
HOW TEXTING CAN HELP

Many self-smart children appear to be shy and quiet, especially when they're in crowds or with a new group of peers. As a result, it may appear that they don't need to be wanted. That's not true, though, as every person is born with a need to belong and connect with others. These children need you to help them find friends rather than just telling them to have friends.

Children with self-smart strengths may greatly appreciate texting and communicating through social media. These don't require the same social intensity as face-to-face communication. And, since they don't have the same strengths in reading body language as people-smart children do, they're at a disadvantage when talking with them. Texting can level the playing field.

Self-smart can be paralyzed when children constantly hear feedback such as, *"Get your head out of that book,"* *"You're being selfish again,"* *"Don't you have anyone to play with?"* or *"You're such a loner!"* Children may begin to believe these negative comments.

Self-smart children usually think of themselves and their own ideas before they think of others. And they think deeply inside of themselves about those ideas so they're often quiet even when in groups. They also like being alone. All of this can cause others to judge them as selfish, self-centered, and unfriendly. Peers may find their quiet and deep thinking intimidating or confusing.

Self-smart children tell me my teaching is freeing and they're grateful to know the roots of their need to be alone and quiet.

Self-smart children may meet their need for belonging through individual sports and activities they can do alone, yet while in a group. Cross-country, tennis, and swimming are sports that may appeal more to self-smart children than sports like volleyball, basketball, and football. Being a photographer for the yearbook and being in charge of posting flyers for the youth retreat may also be appealing.

Relating to Parents: "What Do *You* Think?"

If you want your self-smart children to trust you, you need to know them. This can be challenging because they don't necessarily share a lot. Nevertheless, it's essential. You'll make more progress when your input fits them well. So pay attention to them. Watch and listen. Interact as you can. Let them know you want to talk and be available when they might be in the mood to talk. This might include while you're running errands, because they can talk without needing to make eye contact, and as you put them to bed, because the dark often makes it easier to bring up significant issues.

You'll also want to give them time to reflect, think, and feel before, during, and after discussions about important topics like discipline, motivation, homework, and faith. Valuing their thoughts, and telling them you do, is very important.

Asking your children for their thoughts and recommendations also honors them. Again, just like with people-smart children, self-smart children need the maturity to understand that you don't need to accept all their suggestions. You will listen and work to understand their perspective. This, of course, needs to go both ways. If you listen respectfully to your children's conclusions and recommendations, they need to listen to yours.

SPIRITUAL GROWTH

Silence, Meditation, Journaling . . .

Self-smart children benefit from knowing that God knows their thoughts. Although it's not important to them that *you* know their thoughts, I encourage you to do what you can to engage them in conversations about spiritual things. Don't give up.

Many children with self-smart strengths have deep connections with God. But just as much of the rest of their lives are private, their relationship with God may be very private. You can hope that, at the right time, when the mood and reasons are right, your self-smart children will talk about God with you. You may want to try journaling back and forth because this method will appear to be more private and less intrusive than conversations. You'll need to be vulnerable and transparent for the journaling to be successful. This should eventually lead to face-to-face enjoyable conversations.

Self-smart children may prefer studying Scripture and spiritual books during quiet times rather than in family devotions. However, they'll struggle to have their own devotions if they can't find Scriptures and/or books they can relate to. Self-smart children may enjoy journaling their thoughts and prayers. The disciplines of silence and meditation will also appeal to them. These enhance their power—reflection and the knowing that comes from it.

Personal testimonies can reach self-smart children. They may pay close attention to these during church services, Christian school chapels, children's church, and youth group. They'll learn by trying to put themselves into the speakers' shoes. It might be even more beneficial when you invite people into your home to enjoy a meal with you and share their stories. As they share, your self-smart child will be pondering and learning. In the safety of your family, your child may be willing to ask important follow-up questions.

CHARACTER:
BE SMART WITH YOUR SELF-SMART

Learning Humility

Self-smart children can be very independent and are often content being alone. Therefore, they can become self-centered. Some develop an "It's all about me!" attitude to life.

Pride in their own ideas and in their ability to explain their ideas are possible sins self-smart children need to guard against. They can also believe their ideas are more important than anyone else's. These are tendencies of logic-smart children, too, so if your self-smart child is also quite logic smart, it's especially important to watch for, talk about, and pray against these tendencies.

Self-smart children admit they can struggle to remain open to other people's ideas. Their self-knowledge and deep thinking causes them to be satisfied with what they know. Moreover, until they have time to think about other ideas, whether from pastors, parents, teachers, or in textbooks, they tend to be skeptical. Some have admitted to being unteachable. Others tell me they're not, but they admit to often behaving as if they are.

Many self-smart children value self-discipline. They develop high standards for themselves. When they make mistakes or "mess up," they can be very hard on themselves. Being critical, coupled with being alone and not seeking other people's input, can result in hopelessness and fear.

THE COMBINATION OF PEOPLE-SMART AND SELF-SMART STRENGTHS

There may be no more important smart combination to under-stand than the people-smart/self-smart combination. Think about yourself, your children, and other adults to whom you're close. Any who have both of these in their top four may live in an almost constant state of internal stress and confusion. But understanding these smarts can free you and others to take advantage of the gift and power of this combination.

I often explain it this way: People who have both people-smart and self-smart strengths may be the life of the party on a Friday night. Their people smart was activated and taking the lead. They connected to most of the people. They were able to help some people have a better time by determining their mood, discerning what could change it, and then following through. They had a genuinely great time and said they'd be back the next Friday night.

One week later, they felt obligated to go to the party even though they weren't really in the mood. Maybe they heard something on the radio, were asked a question by a teacher or coworker, or read a Bible verse that activated their self-smart thinking. They would have preferred to stay home where it was quiet and where they'd have space and privacy. Instead, they went to the party. But they stood by themselves and didn't really connect to anyone.

Soon after arriving, a friend approached:

"Are you okay? You're so quiet."

"Yeah, I'm fine."

Ten minutes later, the same person asks, *"Are you sure you're okay? You can talk with me, you know."*

"I'm fine. Don't worry about it."

Ten minutes later, the same person stops by again. *"Have I upset you or something? You seem distant."*

"I told you I'm fine! Just leave me alone!"

Is it any wonder that people with high people-smart and self-smart abilities confuse themselves and others? They're equally skilled at bouncing ideas off others and thinking deeply within themselves. They know themselves well and they know others well, too. They're comfortable with people and alone. Therefore, at times they don't know where to go or who to be!

When I teach high school students about this internal conflict, many cry and thank me for helping them understand themselves. They tell me they thought they were crazy and in need of counseling. They tell me about conflicts with friends, parents, and siblings who complain they're inconsistent and hard to figure out.

In the middle of my explanation of this phenomenon, some teens have actually shouted out, *"That's my mother!"* Then others laugh and point to themselves to indicate they think they have at least one parent with this double strength.

In one-on-one conversations, teens tell me they've thought they were the problem. I've heard about how they come home from school one day and their mom wants to hear all about their day. Then the next day, they're greeted with, *"Not now. Can't you find something to do?"* I help them understand that several things can cause these different reactions, including high people-smart and self-smart intelligences. They're empowered now to give their parents some space if they discern they're in self-smart mode and engage them in conversations when they determine their people-smart skills are ruling. How freeing!

This combination can be very confusing so I encourage you to talk with children about this if it's relevant. It's a very important combination because the self-smart part of them knows things deeply and the people-smart part is confident enough to share the knowledge. We can't afford for either one of these strengths to be paralyzed by lack of use or rejection because it's too confusing. These children may be especially equipped to influence people. Parent them well!

Let's Play!

Do quiet things together that your child chooses, such as completing a puzzle, coloring, building with Legos, playing with dolls, or playing a car game like "Who Am I?"

A FINAL WORD

I hope you've been deeply encouraged by these truths and have enjoyed learning about them. Isn't God generous to have created us with so many smarts! I pray putting ideas into practice is already going well and continues to be a blessing.

Let me remind you one more time to use the interactive online tool we designed to help you track these smarts.

NOTES

Chapter 1—"How Am I Smart?" An Introduction to the Eight Great Smarts

1. "Right Brain, Left Brain? Scientists Debunk Popular Theory," *Huffington Post*, August 20, 2013, http://www.huffingtonpost.com/2013/08/19/right-brain-left-brain-debunked_n_3762322.html. See also Kendra Cherry, "Left Brain vs. Right Brain: Understanding the Myth of Left Brain and Right Brain Dominance," *About Education*, http://psychology.about.com/od/cognitive-psychology/a/left-brain-right-brain.htm. See also Remy Melina, "What's the Difference between the Right Brain and Left Brain?", *LiveScience*, January 12, 2011, http://www.livescience.com/32935-whats-the-difference-between-the-right-brain-and-left-brain.html. See also J. A. Nielsen, B. A. Zielinski, M. A. Ferguson, J. E. Lainhart & J. S. Anderson, *PLOS ONE*, "An Evaluation of the Left-Brain vs. Right Brain Hypothesis with Resting State Functional Connectivity Magnetic Resonance Imaging," August 14, 2013, http://journals.plos.org/plosone/article?id=10.1371/journal.pone.0071275.

2. If you're interested in knowing Dr. Gardner's criteria for categorizing something as an "intelligence" versus a skill or talent, please see his 1993 book, *Frames of Mind: The Theory of Multiple Intelligences* Tenth-Anniversary Edition (London: Fontana Press), 62–67.

3. H. Gardner, "Reflections on Multiple Intelligences: Myths and Messages," *Phi Delta Kappan* 77, no. 3 (1995): 203.

4. "Making Connections—Wiring the Brain," Better Brains for Babies, University of Georgia, 2014, http://spock.fcs.uga.edu.

5. Ibid.

6. Kathy Koch, *Screens and Teens: Connecting with Our Kids in a Wireless World* (Chicago: Moody, 2015), 33–34.

7. James Hamblin, "100 Percent Is Overrated," *The Atlantic*, June 30, 2015, http://www.theatlantic.com/education/archive/2015/06/the-s-word/397205/. See also Salman Khan, "The Learning Myth: Why I'll Never Tell My Son He's Smart," *Huffington Post*, August 19, 2014, http://www.huffingtonpost.com/salman-khan/the-learning-myth-why-ill_b_5691681.html. See also Headmistress/Zookeeper, "Don't Tell Your Kids They're Smart," *The Common Room Blog,* September 25, 2013, http://thecommonroomblog.com/2013/09/dont-tell-your-kids-theyre-smart.html. See also Alexandra Ossola, "Too Many Kids Quit Science Because They Don't Think They're Smart," *The Atlantic*, November 3, 2014, http://www.theatlantic.com/education/archive/2014/11/too-many-kids-quit-science-because-they-dont-think-theyre-smart/382165/.

8. For a complete and practical explanation of these five core needs, I encourage you to read my first book: *Finding Authentic Hope and Wholeness: 5 Questions That Will Change Your Life* (Chicago: Moody, 2005). There's also a summary of how God meets our core needs posted on our website: www.8GreatSmarts.com.

Chapter 2—"I Will Be Smart with My Smarts!" Multiple Intelligences and Character Intersect

1. Correcting children well isn't easy—it's a fine art. This topic is covered in chapters 6 and 9 in *No More Perfect Kids*. I also offer a CD, *Fabulous Feedback: Complimenting and Correcting Children,* on our website: www.CelebrateKids.com.

2. Jill Savage and Kathy Koch, *No More Perfect Kids: Love Your Kids for Who They Are* (Chicago: Moody, 2014).

3. Ibid.

4. Carol Dweck, *Mindset: The New Psychology of Success* (New York: Ballantine Books, 2007).

Chapter 3—I Am Word Smart: I Think with Words

1. Savage and Koch, *No More Perfect Kids.*

2. Dweck, *Mindset.*

3. See appendix A for ways word-smart children may learn vocabulary definitions well.

4. Koch, *Screens and Teens,* see especially chapter 6.

5. Ibid., 42–44.

6. An extensive list of job skills and sample professions for each of the eight smarts is available here: www.8GreatSmarts.com.

7. Savage and Koch, *No More Perfect Kids*, chapter 3.

Chapter 4—I Am Logic Smart: I Think with Questions

1. See appendix B for a list of thinking verbs to teach and use with your children.

2. See appendix A for ways logic-smart children may learn vocabulary definitions well.

3. Savage and Koch, *No More Perfect Kids.*

Chapter 5—I Am Picture Smart: I Think with My Eyes

1. Koch, *Screens and Teens.*

2. You can learn more about this program for all math facts at www.CityCreek.com.

3. See appendix A for ways picture-smart children may learn vocabulary definitions well.

4. Appendix B, first mentioned in chapter 4, has a complete list of thinking verbs. You'll find verbs here that will work well with picture-smart children.

5. Check out the Picture-Smart Bible at www.PictureSmartBible.com. It's one of my highest recommendations because every book of the Bible is beautifully and accurately summarized in a half- or full-page visual. While you read from a prepared script, children trace pictures representing key elements in the book and then color them however they want. You can do it, too. This tracing transfers the image to the brain and is used by God to renew the mind. I'm not very picture smart, but I like this approach because it activates a weaker smart I normally don't use. Added to my strengths, it enhances my comprehension and retention of the book's themes. Children who have picture-smart strengths can really benefit from and enjoy this Bible. You can use it for family devotions, your homeschool curriculum, or other appropriate platforms in your church or school.

Chapter 6—I Am Music Smart: I Think with Rhythms and Melodies

1. Quoted in Joan Peyser, *The Memory of All That: The Life of George Gershwin* (New York: Simon and Schuster, 1993), 80.

2. See appendix A for ways music-smart children may learn vocabulary definitions well.

3. Savage and Koch, *No More Perfect Kids.*

Chapter 7—I Am Body Smart: I Think with Movement and Touch

1. Savage and Koch, *No More Perfect Kids.*

2. See appendix A for ways body-smart children may learn vocabulary definitions well.

Chapter 8—I Am Nature Smart: I Think with Patterns

1. See appendix B for a list of thinking verbs. Use these strategically to help nature-smart children.

2. See appendix A for ways nature-smart children may learn vocabulary definitions well.

3. Savage and Koch, *No More Perfect Kids*, 65–66.

Chapter 9—I Am People Smart: I Think with People

1. Carol Bainbridge, "Extrovert," *About Parenting*, http://giftedkids.about.com/od/glossary/g/extrovert.htm.

2. Carol Bainbridge, "Introvert," *About Parenting*, http://giftedkids.about.com/od/glossary/g/introvert.htm.

3. See appendix A for ways people-smart children may learn vocabulary definitions well.

4. Bainbridge, "Introvert," *About Parenting*.

Chapter 10—I Am Self-Smart: I Think with Reflection

1. Bainbridge, "Extrovert," *About Parenting*.

2. Bainbridge, "Introvert," *About Parenting*.

3. See appendix A for ways self-smart children may learn vocabulary definitions well.

APPENDIX A:
LEARNING VOCABULARY DEFINITIONS
WITH ALL EIGHT SMARTS

Children of all ages need to know vocabulary. When they don't know the words they hear and the words they read, their learning will suffer. Because of the importance of vocabulary development, I provide suggestions here for learning words with all eight smarts. But you can do more with these suggestions. With just a few adaptations, you can use these ideas when your children are learning math facts, spelling words, the order of events for a history assignment, and more. Let these ideas be just the beginning.

Don't use all these ideas on one day. That will be too much and add to your children's confusion. Rather, think in terms of learning over time. They can study words with one smart one night and another one on a different night. You may want to always use their strong smarts. Using their weaker intelligences, too, means more of their mind is involved so that can add strength to their learning. All of us can use all eight smarts; some just take more effort and reminders.

For example:

Word Smart—Read the definition to them and have them read it to you with great expression. Talk about the word and its definition using rich, descriptive language. Use the word in conversation when you can. Have them write the word in sentences that prove they know the meaning of the word. Use a variety of paper, pens, and pencils. Have children find the word in books, online sources, and media. It sometimes works to discuss synonyms, antonyms, and words that are similar, but different.

Logic Smart—Asking and answering questions about the words is the most obvious use of logic smart. You can ask about the word, its part of speech, and definition in a variety of ways. Ask what words they can think of that are similar or very different. Talk about what is logical and what is illogical regarding the words' spelling and meaning. Researching the words' origin and uses may be helpful and interesting.

Picture Smart—Ask children what pictures they see in their minds when thinking about the words. Encourage them to visualize the definition of the words in great detail. You can start explanations and discussions about the words with, "Picture this…" and then ask them what they saw. Have them sketch/

draw definitions on paper, too. Children can find pictures that illustrate the words' meanings. Challenge them to write/draw the letters of the word in a way that each letter or the final result relates to the meaning of the word somehow.

Music Smart—Just like we have all learned to spell "Mississippi" with a rhythm and we remember the order of the ABCs with a melody, children can learn other words and their definitions with rhythms and melodies. They can also add more music by clapping or tapping the rhythms or melodies as they say the definitions. Changing volume can be effective, too. At home, when studying, they can shout the most important part of the definition. Even whispering it can help them remember it. Sometimes finding music that illustrates the meaning of words is very effective and enjoyable.

Body Smart—Have children act out the definitions. Use role-plays and charades. They could pretend to be a mime as they try to express the definition with action. Saying the definition while skywriting it by making the letters as large as possible, as if they're painting the sky to involve more muscles, can help. They can also march, taking a step for each word in the definition, to help the body remember. Using manipulatives like magnetic letters on the refrigerator while spelling the word and saying the definition can help.

Nature Smart—Pointing out patterns in the words and their definitions will help. This can include how the words and definitions are similar and different to others. When studying more than one word, organizing them in a particular pattern they choose may help. Relating the words to nature, when possible, will help children to remember them.

People Smart—Talking with others about the words and their definitions helps activate this smart. They can use words in a variety of sentences and tell stories about the words. They can include planned and purposeful debates and brainstorming. They can exaggerate their use of language when reciting definitions out loud, as if they're on a stage performing in a play, to add to their memory.

Self-Smart—Taking time for deep, quiet thinking is essential. Doing this where it's quiet is smart. Any way they can relate the words to their lives will help them be remembered. Using words they choose in the definition, if they're personal and accurate, rather than just the words out of a book or dictionary may be wise. Thinking of personal reasons the words are important may help.

APPENDIX B: THINKING VERBS

Children's smarts influence which thinking verbs they most naturally use. For instance, those with logic-smart strengths will usually think about things first in order to analyze, sequence, and solve. Children with self-smart strengths may decide, reflect, and give an example. Picture-smart children will most easily describe, illustrate, and design. To be successful in school and in life, it helps if children are exposed to and somewhat comfortable with all these verbs. You'll want to use a variety during family discussions and while teaching and on assignments, if you homeschool your children.

Using different verbs in a timely and strategic manner can help awaken the smarts. Using them on assignments and encouraging children to use them when studying on their own can improve their comprehension, memory, and ability to use the information accurately.

Start with teaching what these verbs mean. You can choose the ones that are age-appropriate for your children and actually assign them as vocabulary words. What are the differences between compare and contrast? Between judge and evaluate? For the words that are very similar, explain when one might be used more appropriately than another. These efforts can help children predict questions teachers may use on tests so they're better prepared. They can also use relevant verbs when thinking about what information to include in papers and presentations. This will enhance their work.

agree	diagram	judge	relate
analyze	disagree	justify	reorganize
apply	discuss	label	restate
choose	distinguish	list	review
classify	evaluate	modify	select
combine	examine	name	sequence
compare	explain	outline	show
condense	extend	paraphrase	simplify
contrast	find	ponder	solve
create	formulate	predict	speculate
decide	generalize	prioritize	state
defend	give an example	produce	summarize
define	give cause/effect	prove	support
demonstrate	identify	react	synthesize
describe	illustrate	rearrange	trace
design	infer	record	transfer
determine	interpret	reflect	use

ACKNOWLEDGMENTS

Writing this book reminded me of many rich childhood experiences. I'm grateful for my parents' love, support, and interest. I wouldn't be who I am without their total investment. I wouldn't be doing what I'm doing. God provided the nature and they, my brother, extended family, teachers, and friends provided nurture. I have always been surrounded by fabulous people and I'm grateful.

The practical, emotional, and prayer support from my staff and Board of Directors has been essential. Without them and my church family and numerous friends, I couldn't accomplish what I do. Men and women I've met through my work enrich my life. I'm thankful for those in my audiences and those I share stages with.

I also appreciate being represented by Ambassadors Speakers Bureau. Their work on my behalf allows me to influence thousands of parents, teachers, teens, and others through presentations. Of course, without the talented and passionate team of people from Moody Publishers who worked with me on this book, it wouldn't exist. They inspire me!

I'm grateful to God for choosing to create me and to create me the way He did. His equipping is so beautiful! (I hope this book has helped you say the same.) I live in light of Jesus' sacrifice to save me. I will be forever grateful. I'm also grateful for God's gift of the Holy Spirit and His comfort and guidance.

Celebrate Kids, Inc. is dedicated to helping especially parents, educators, and children of all ages meet their core needs of security, identity, belonging, purpose, and competence in healthy ways. Through a problem-solving framework of these integrated needs, our programs and products provide solution-focused strategies that improve their intellectual, emotional, social, physical, and spiritual health.

Celebrate Kids helps parents, grandparents, teachers, administrators, pastors, and those who volunteer with children understand today's children and teens, value them, and help them use their strengths only for good and not to do harm.

Through live presentations in churches, schools, and conventions; an extensive product line; our social media presence; and our biweekly email newsletter, we offer authentic hope for today and tomorrow and relevant solutions that work.

Dr. Kathy Koch founded Celebrate Kids in 1991, after serving as an elementary teacher, middle school coach, school board member, and university professor. Originally from Wauwatosa, a Milwaukee, WI, suburb, she moved to Fort Worth, TX, from Green Bay, WI, to fulfill God's purposes for her.

Email: Smarts@CelebrateKids.com

Website: www.CelebrateKids.com

Blog: www.DrKathyKoch.com

Video: www.vimeo.com/channels/kathyisms

Facebook: www.facebook.com/celebratekidsinc

Twitter: @DrKathyKoch

Website for this book: www.8GreatSmarts.com